'In our era of mass migration and segregation, when new categories of otherness are invented to dehumanize and control, Daniel Bristow tackles the divisions and antagonisms that structure our unconscious, showing how our split subjectivities are ripe for revolutionary futures. Creatively appropriating Hegel's *Aufhebung* by way of Lacan, this concise and cogent book brings together psychoanalysis, structuralism, and Marxism. Opening the possibility of reading Freud, Reich and Laing together, Bristow performs a surgically precise topological cut that transforms what it unites and separates. An important and timely book for anyone interested in the political unconscious.'

Patricia Gherovici, *Psychoanalyst and Author,*
Recipient of the 2020 Sigourney Award

'There is no sharper analyst of Lacanian topologies than Daniel Bristow. In this elegant, concise and original book, following his outstanding work on Joyce and Lacan, he performs a Marxism of schizo-analysis, and a schizo-analysis of Marxism. He thus rescues the term "schizo-" from its normative encrustations, and restores its power as a dialectical principle.'

Richard Seymour, *Author of* The Twittering
Machine *(Verso, 2020)*

'Despite its brevity, this book offers a rich and intricate exploration of the question of dis/continuity and change, in spatial, temporal and social terms, building with originality upon key contributions in understanding the nature of the mind, as elaborated over the last century in psychoanalysis, from Freud to Lacan, and beyond. This exploration raises important questions about the nature and emergence of psychic structures, not just in theory, but in the reality of a less than perfect world.'

A. Carrington, *Analyst*

'Bristow has crafted a creative tool for Lacanian studies which others can mold to their academic and clinical experiences. A medium serving multiple creative environments is indispensable—and its creation is testament to Bristow's confluential sensibilities.'

S. Alfonso Williams, *Independent Researcher*
and Interlocutor

Schizostructuralism

Schizostructuralism draws together insights from psychoanalytic, structuralist, and Marxist theory, and the divisions and antagonisms that both underpin and distinguish them, to form a new psychoanalytic system.

Working through the key concepts and methods in these fields, Daniel Bristow describes the processes of unification and separation inherent in structure; extends concepts within the field of psychoanalytic topology and its study of surface; and interrogates types and phasings of time that operate psychosocially, testing workings of these against analyses of class division and struggle. Returning to and working through key concepts and methods in the fields of structuralism, topology, temporality, and Marxist political theory, *Schizostructuralism* looks again at such major figures as Freud, Reich, Lacan, Laing, and Deleuze and Guattari—invoking their socially oriented theories and practices—and sets out possibilities for recalibrating critical and clinical approaches to be more politically radical and inclusive. Bristow draws on an array of schematic diagrams, depicting and formulating the clinical categories of neurosis, perversion, and psychosis.

Schizostructuralism will be of interest to academics and students of psychoanalytic studies, Lacanian studies, and philosophy. It will also inform psychoanalysts in practice and in training.

Daniel Bristow is a psychoanalytic theorist and practitioner completing his formation with the Philadelphia Association. He is the author of *Joyce and Lacan: Reading, Writing, and Psychoanalysis* (Routledge).

The Lines of the Symbolic in Psychoanalysis Series
Series Editor: Ian Parker, *Manchester Psychoanalytic Matrix*

Psychoanalytic clinical and theoretical work is always embedded in specific linguistic and cultural contexts and carries their traces, traces which this series attends to in its focus on multiple contradictory and antagonistic 'lines of the Symbolic'. This series takes its cue from Lacan's psychoanalytic work on three registers of human experience, the Symbolic, the Imaginary and the Real, and employs this distinctive understanding of culture, communication and embodiment to link with other traditions of cultural, clinical and theoretical practice beyond the Lacanian symbolic universe. *The Lines of the Symbolic in Psychoanalysis Series* provides a reflexive reworking of theoretical and practical issues, translating psychoanalytic writing from different contexts, grounding that work in the specific histories and politics that provide the conditions of possibility for its descriptions and interventions to function. The series makes connections between different cultural and disciplinary sites in which psychoanalysis operates, questioning the idea that there could be one single correct reading and application of Lacan. Its authors trace their own path, their own line through the Symbolic, situating psychoanalysis in relation to debates which intersect with Lacanian work, explicating it, extending it and challenging it.

Lacan and Critical Feminism
Subjectivity, Sexuation, and Discourse
Rahna McKey Carusi

Schizostructuralism
Divisions in Structure, Surface, Temporality, Class
Daniel Bristow

Obscenity, Psychoanalysis and Literature
Lawrence and Joyce on Trial
William Simms

Schizostructuralism

Divisions in Structure, Surface,
Temporality, Class

Daniel Bristow

LONDON AND NEW YORK

First published 2022
by Routledge
2 Park Square, Milton Park, Abingdon, Oxon OX14 4RN

and by Routledge
605 Third Avenue, New York, NY 10158

Routledge is an imprint of the Taylor & Francis Group, an informa business

© 2022 Daniel Bristow

British Library Cataloguing-in-Publication Data
A catalogue record for this book is available from the British Library

Library of Congress Cataloging-in-Publication Data
Names: Bristow, Daniel, author.
Title: Schizostructuralism : divisions in structure, surface, temporality, class / Daniel Bristow.
Description: Abingdon, Oxon ; New York, NY : Routledge, 2022. | Series: The lines of the symbolic in psychoanalysis series | Includes bibliographical references and index. | Identifiers: LCCN 2021010344 (print) | LCCN 2021010345 (ebook) | ISBN 9781032027975 (hbk) | ISBN 9781032058726 (pbk) | ISBN 9781003185239 (ebk)
Subjects: LCSH: Psychoanalysis. | Structuralism. | Communism. | Socialism.
Classification: LCC BF173 .B822 2022 (print) | LCC BF173 (ebook) | DDC 150.19/5–dc23
LC record available at https://lccn.loc.gov/2021010344
LC ebook record available at https://lccn.loc.gov/2021010345

ISBN: 978-1-032-02797-5 (hbk)
ISBN: 978-1-032-05872-6 (pbk)
ISBN: 978-1-003-18523-9 (ebk)

DOI: 10.4324/9781003185239

Typeset in Times New Roman
by Newgen Publishing UK

To Tamara

Contents

Series editor preface

What would psychoanalysis look like that took structure seriously, that also worked its way through the impossible contradictions that ensure that this structure fails, repeatedly fails, and repeatedly shores itself up? It would, this book shows in a rigorous dialectical reading of key concepts, be the psychoanalysis of Freud and Lacan, yes, but now interrogated and unraveled and stitched together again in such a way as to embed them in triple-lock domains of structure that make of them revolutionary approaches to society in crisis as much as to an individual in analysis.

Here Wilhelm Reich is reminder of the Marxist class critique that accompanied Freudian theory, and who sharpened it against the attempts to turn psychoanalysis into false balm, into therapeutic solace for material oppression. Reich's internal critique was a 'cut', an interruption, a question about what psychoanalysis that individualized distress was complicit in. And then Laing and Esterson, who refused the normative and pathologising weight of the label 'schizo' in psychiatric and psychoanalytic practice, cut into psychoanalysis again; now, in a rereading of the Blairs and the Heads, we have an exploration of schizophrenogenic family systems that treat these systems not as a 'systemic' therapist would, but in a way that really does treat them as structure, structure reproducing patriarchy and class, and as always already riven by contradictions, cuts, 'enverneous'.

Daniel Bristow's *Schizostructuralism* retrieves what is necessarily irremediably 'schizo' about structuralism by cutting through and reassembling elements of its history, and that also requires reflexive looping around the weird topologies of subjectivity that make Freud and Lacan, and, it turns out, Marx, so psychoanalytic. This is where the triple-lock of Symbolic, Imaginary, and Real is dismantled in such a way as to help us see how forms of capital are reproduced through class, family structure, and in the interior of the Freudian subject. The Real here is the always hidden, ineluctable precondition for the divided, fractured Symbolic conditions for our speech and for the Imaginary attempt to make things whole, for the very split between Symbolic and Imaginary that makes subjectivity possible, and so impossible.

Psychoanalytic clinical and theoretical work circulates through multiple intersecting antagonistic symbolic universes. This series opens connections between different cultural sites in which Lacanian work has developed in distinctive ways, in forms of work that question the idea that there could be a single correct reading and application. The Lines of the Symbolic in Psychoanalysis series provides a reflexive reworking of psychoanalysis that transmits Lacanian writing from around the world, steering a course between the temptations of a metalanguage and imaginary reduction, between the claim to provide a god's eye view of psychoanalysis and the idea that psychoanalysis must everywhere be the same. And the elaboration of psychoanalysis in the symbolic here grounds its theory and practice in the history and politics of the work in a variety of interventions that touch the real.

Ian Parker
Manchester Psychoanalytic Matrix

Acknowledgements

A great many people are owed thanks for every form of encouragement and assistance during the processes of composing and compositing this book. Particular gratitude to Ian Parker for welcoming this work into this wonderful series; at Routledge: to Alexis O'Brien, Susannah Frearson, Ellie Duncan, and Lizzie Cox; to Kawiya Bakthavatchalam and the Newgen team; and to the members of my topology reading cartel: Anca Carrington, Hephzibah Rendle-Short, and Stefan Marianski.

Introduction: 'Schizostructuralism'

'Schizo-' is a combinative word—deriving from the Greek '*σχίζειν*' ('*skhizein*')—meaning 'to split'. It is a signifier into which has been poured a great many excesses of mental pathologisation and psychical stigmatisation, a playground taunt often neither playful nor grounded, nor tethered to an institutional or empirical knowledge. In the press release for the (in)famous 'Schizo-Culture' conference—held at Columbia University, New York, in November 1975, and featuring, amongst a host of others, Gilles Deleuze, Félix Guattari, and R. D. Laing, as well as discussion of Sigmund Freud, Wilhelm Reich, and Jacques Lacan—the definition leant to the title's prefix did 'not refer here to any clinical entity, but to the *process* by which social controls of all kinds, endlessly re-imposed by capitalism, are broken up and opened to revolutionary change' (to which theme this work returns, in its analyses and formations).[1]

When attempts have been made to found a *clinical* knowledge, this itself has often receded. The psychoanalysis of Freud led a way to it, and led away from it, pulling up short of accompanying its clinicians into the unpromised land.[2] Lacan's 'return to Freud' formulated a practice in which the theory of the psychoses—of which schizophrenia might be called a 'dialect'—found its redux in the psychoanalytic setting. If the frenetic world of Deleuze and Guattari's 'schizoanalysis' is an '*in medias res*', Laing's measured sittings-with and listenings-to are a bridge, mindful—and maintainative—of what it separates and unites.[3] From his clinical work in the practice of character analysis, which he adapted out of Freud's founding methodologies, Reich—radical communist physician, and star pupil of, then exile from, Freud's Vienna school—confirmed revolutionary openings with the words: 'I found my liking of the schizoid mind again justified. Schizophrenics are able in their lucid periods to see through individual and social matters intelligently, as no other character type can.'[4]

DOI: 10.4324/9781003185239-1

It is a lucidity we attempt here to build into and pull out of the theoretical edifices of psychoanalysis, structuralism, and Marxism, excavating the very splits—divisions and antagonisms—out of which they grow and become animated, *unify*, and *separate*, and which rivet and riven them. In the attempt, we might hope to decathect the word 'schizo-' of some of its prejudicial and *othering* investments; and to posit something of, and derive something from, a missed encounter, between structuralism and the 'schizoanalytic' project—too readily projected into a *beyond*; that of 'poststructuralism'—through an archaeology of divisions: in structure, surface, temporality, class struggle. Through this, the aim is to rediscover in, and through, dialectical materialism, and psychoanalysis, what Ambalavaner Sivanandan so beautifully described as 'a way of understanding how conflict itself [i]s the motor of one's personal life as well as the combusting force of the society in which one live[s]'.[5]

This short book is the culmination of a decade-long engagement with psychoanalytic, structuralist, and Marxist theory; it draws together and adapts other published work, and strands therein, and combines these with original material, building a new organ out of dispersed bodies, and around a systematic skeletal architecture; its chapters each represent a condensation of the workings of a theory or concept. Chapter 1, that of *enverity*, describes the processes of unification and separation inherent in *structure*. Chapter 2 extends concepts within the field of psychoanalytic topology, and its study of *surface*. It relies on an array of schematic diagrams, depicting and formulating the clinical categories: of neurosis, perversion, and psychosis. These schematisations merit some meditation and can be practically studied—if one so wishes—by modelling them from strips of paper and lengths of string (or pipe cleaners, which are specially suited to their formulation). Chapter 3 moves from space into time, via the theory of *enverneity*, which extends that of *enverity* to disjunctures in *temporality*, and interrogates types and phasings of time that operate psychosocially. Chapter 4 tests the workings of the previous against analyses of class division, and struggle, working through notions of primary and secondary process, and arraying aspects of class distinction and differentiation against the three orders of the tripartite psychoanalytic system of Real, Symbolic, and Imaginary. The hope is to forge an appreciation of divisions and antagonisms that go to structure the strange spaces and times of the unconscious, and its psychality; of subjectivity, and its revolutionary horizons.

Notes

1 'Schizo-Culture: A "Revolution in Desire"' [1975], in *Schizo-Culture: The Event, 1975*, ed. by Sylvère Lotringer and David Morris (South Pasadena: Semiotext(e), 2013) p.7. The conference was itself an extraordinary event of 'desiring-production'—in practice and in output—through which all the flows and fluidities, connections and pluggings-in, meldings and blendings, breakings and ruptures (in short, so many 'rhizomatic' elements that would become a veritable 'schizocultural' assemblage) came together, in colloquia revolving around the revolutionary potentials, intersections, and schisms, within discourses and theories; of feminism, antipsychiatry, anti-racism, anti-capitalism.

2 In his study of Paul Daniel Schreber (a German judge—deemed schizophrenic—who wrote an account of his mental illness, from which Freud conducted his case study), Freud stated: "schizophrenia' [is] open to the objection that the name appears appropriate only so long as we forget its literal meaning ['split mind']. For otherwise it prejudices the issue, since it is based on a character-istic of the disease which is theoretically postulated—a characteristic, more-over, which does not belong exclusively to that disease, and which, in the light of other considerations, cannot be regarded as the essential one.' See Sigmund Freud, 'Psycho-Analytic Notes on an Autobiographical Account of a Case of Paranoia (Dementia Paranoides)' [1911], trans. by Alix and James Strachey, in *The Standard Edition of the Complete Psychological Works of Sigmund Freud, Volume XII (1911–1913): Case History of Schreber, Papers on Technique and Other Works*, ed. by James Strachey, with Anna Freud, assisted by Alix Strachey and Alan Tyson, 24 vols (London: Vintage, 2001) XII, p.75. The *Standard Edition* of Freud's works will hereafter be referred to as *SE*, followed by volume then page number. The integrality of splitting (*Spaltung*), or division, across all clinical or subjective structures, becomes more apparent in Freud's late works, 'Splitting of the Ego in the Process of Defence' (1940), and *An Outline of Psycho-Analysis* (1940), both included in SE, XXIII. It subsequently founds Lacan's key theory of division as being at the heart of the subject.

3 Laing and Aaron Esterson state: 'we do not accept 'schizophrenia' as being a biochemical, neurophysiological, psychological fact, and we regard it as palpable error, in the present state of the evidence, to take it to be a fact. Nor do we assume its existence. Nor do we adopt it as a hypothesis. We propose no model for it.

This is the position from which we start. Our question is: are the experi-ence and behaviour that psychiatrists take as symptoms and signs of schizo-phrenia more socially intelligible than has come to be supposed?' See R. D. Laing and Aaron Esterson, 'Preface to the Second Edition', in *Sanity, Madness and the Family: Families of Schizophrenics* [1964] (Abingdon: Routledge Classics, 2017) p.xvii. Against the Pharisaism of the 'psy-complex', Deleuze and Guattari beautifully state in *Anti-Oedipus*: 'someone asked us once if we had ever seen a schizophrenic – no, no, we have never seen one.' See Gilles

Deleuze and Félix Guattari, *Anti-Oedipus: Capitalism and Schizophrenia, Vol. 1* [1972], trans. by Robert Hurley, Mark Seem, and Helen R. Lane (London: Continuum, 2004) p.415.

4 Wilhelm Reich, *Character Analysis* [1933/1945], trans. by Vincent D. Carfagno (New York: Noonday Press, 1990) p.413.

5 A. Sivanandan, 'The Heart Is Where the Battle Is: An Interview with the Author', in *Communities of Resistance: Writings on Black Struggles for Socialism* (London: Verso, 2019) p.5.

1 Enverity

(Divisions in structure: the unconscious)[1]

Unificatory/Separatoriness

In the 1952 interview known as 'Reich Speaks of Freud', the revolutionary Marxist psychoanalyst, and later experimental biologist, Wilhelm Reich said of the founder of psychoanalysis and inventor of the unconscious, Sigmund Freud—of whose libido theory the former remained a dedicated disciple, and became a theoretical expansionist—that he

> was mainly a dialectician, a functionally thinking human being. He always wanted two forces to counteract each other. What he did not do, and I don't know why, was to see that *these two opposite forces were actually one in the depth because everything opposed in nature is ultimately a unit*. Yes, a unit. Do I make myself clear? Of course they split up. Did you see our sign on the observatory? It's over the door. Look at it when you walk out. Are you familiar with the sign? [Figure 1.1] *Out of a unitary force a splitting, an antithesis develops.*[2]

In James E. Strick's recent scientific biography of Reich, he describes the scientist's work as 'from early on characterized by two prominent strands: (1) the concept of simultaneous identity and antithesis and (2) the energy principle'.[3] Strick locates this first concept in Reich's elucidation (as above)

> that two forces imagined to be opposites (an anthesis) could both simultaneously also be manifestations of a common, underlying unified force (thus, in that sense, they constitute an identity). For example, expansion and contraction—apparent opposites— are unified as phases of the unitary act of pulsation (as in the heartbeat).[4]

DOI: 10.4324/9781003185239-2

Figure 1.1 Symbol of orgonomic functionalism.

However, Reich's words in the interview referred especially to what he saw as an epistemological break in Freud's work: his introduction of the concept of the death drive. Reich railed against this theory—and the fact that the majority of Freud's followers uncritically went over to the side of it—advocating in its stead a life-force (which he would come to name 'orgone', and which he firmly set on the side of Eros—in the nomenclature of the Greek gods that the dichotomy came to be known by), one of the manifestations of which—resulting from energetic blockage, and in a splitting—could be a death impulse, instinct, or drive (on the side of Thanatos).

Yet, instead of doing away with it, Reich in fact maintains this binary on which his break with and departure from Freud was based. If he argued against Freud's needing two *separate* principles (the life drive of libido, or Eros, and the death drive (also libidinal), or Thanatos) his identity/antithesis concept does not here actually allow of their unification, but keeps the death drive either split off entirely, or as only able to come about as a distorted manifestation of a 'unitary force' (that of his life energy). Indeed, in Freud's libidinally cathectic topographies of the drives, there is perhaps more scope for the drawing-out of an identity/anthesis principle from the still-present theory of energetics in his descriptions of libido (here thus also mappable as that 'unitary force') throughout his work. Was it that in Freud's attempts at separation he always ran up against ineluctable unification and in Reich's attempts at unification he would come up against necessitous separation? Might it then be that unification and separation themselves are *spliced*; bound together whilst being split asunder? Freud and Reich's theories—almost similar, but riven by minimal difference—seem to thus be simultaneously pushing against and pulling away from one another.

If we read Reich's claims closely, deconstructively, he makes out that Freud always had a desire to postulate counteracting forces, whilst Reich himself would conceptualise of these forces as in fact one, 'in the depth' of a 'natural unity'. Yet, he goes on to say that 'of course they split up', in the grammatics of which sentence he already postulates an *originary* split, in his use of the word 'they' (after his designation of a unit), over 'it'; he acknowledges—albeit disavowedly (or, as if the structure of his enunciation cannot quite articulate its statement)—a counteraction inherent in *unifaction*; the singular force's *plurality*; its twoness in *their* oneness: what we deign to call 'unificatory/separatoriness'. Ergo, if two do not become one, nor one two, it is the *antagonism* between them— that which *unifies and separates* at once—that is foundational, that is the *functor* (that which puts into function) of one and two.

In his late work, Reich came to be an adherent of the philosophy of Giordano Bruno who put forward (and drew out from the work of Nicholas of Cusa) the concept of the 'coincidence of contraries'; instances of unificatory/separatoriness we might thus reterm 'coincidents of contraries'. For Bruno, 'contraries coincide both in principle and reality'.[5] This notion deeply impressed the modernist Irish exiled writer James Joyce, who paraphrased Bruno with the words: 'all power, whether in nature or the spirit, must create an opposing power without which man cannot fulfil himself, and he [Bruno] adds that in every such separation there is a tendency towards a reunion'.[6] This necessitous creation of an opposing power might seem to hark back to Reich's Freud, but it is in fact more in the spirit of Reich's own unitary force, and more akin to the orgonomic symbol (see Figure 1.1). For it is in fact in Freud that we find that 'what we call our 'unconscious'—the deepest strata of our minds, made up of instinctual impulses—knows nothing that is negative, and no negation; in it contradictories coincide'.[7] This coincision thus harbours contraries in their state of primary antagonism or unificatory/ separatoriness; that is, as *at once coincident and contrarian*.

Interestingly, Freud's statement can be read as having been made in a passage in which he denies his very concept of the death-drive before he had come to create it; and yet, a more attentive reading will uncover the interplays involved in the situation of drives within the unconscious:

our unconscious, then, does not believe in its own death; [...] it does not know its own death, for to that we can give only a negative content. Thus there is nothing instinctual in us which responds to a belief in death.[8]

This is the 'short-circuit' of the death-drive, which in its pulsion towards death, in fact sustains life.[9] This is what escapes Reich in regard to the death-drive; that 'in the depth' it operates as the coincident-of-contrary to the life-drive, within the unificatory/separatoriness (the *animating antagonism*) of libido, the cathexes of which the unconscious is constantly sending forth and retracting, or *pulsating* (in the identity-antithesis model).

The disagreement between Freud and Reich remains one of the most fundamental in the history of psychoanalysis, spurring two distinct, extraordinary bodies of work—*from one*, in which for a time contraries were coincident—tendencies towards resistance and reunion of which resurrect and continue.

Whilst establishing both of these thinkers as fundamental to this study, we will, however, situate our concept of unificatory/separatoriness as a *third* discursion, and explore it here through theories of structure.

Enverity

In the book *Joyce and Lacan: Reading, Writing, and Psychoanalysis* (2016) an attempt was made to delineate a concept to which was given the name '*enverity*', and which also went under the moniker the 'unificatory/separatory principle'. At its most fundamental level the purpose of this principle is to demarcate the necessity of separation in all instances of unification, and of unification in all instances of separation, and thus to posit the principal position (that of *functor*) of 'unificatory/separatoriness' within these processes. Diagrammatically—in accord with the schema used throughout the book—this can be conveyed by *unificatory/separatoriness*, *unification*, and *separation* occupying positions A, 1, and 2, respectively, in Figure 1.2, and making that of Figure 1.3:

Figure 1.2 Principle of *enverity*: positions.

Figure 1.3 Positional demonstration: unificatory/separatory principle.

This introductory chapter to this short work—which aims to condense, apply, and extend this concept—will parse, draw on, and develop some of the theoretical advances made within that book, which relied on and explored, the late thought of the psychoanalyst and psychoanalytic theorist Jacques Lacan, and its operation within, ties to, and ventures beyond, structuralist discourse.

The conjugation 'enverity' is derived from the English translation of the French word '*envers*'; its admixture with the term 'verity'; and—through this combination—its being made into an abstract noun, which fulfils the role of *functor* (taken to mean that which sets (a) function(ing) in motion). Lacan's seventeenth Seminar—*L'envers de la Psychanalyse*—was given the English title *The Other Side of Psychoanalysis*. In a translator's note explaining the choice of 'the other side' for '*l'envers*', Russell Grigg states that the word 'also carries the meaning of [...] "verso," "lining," "underside," "flipside," "underneath," "bad side"—connotations of the unseen, even the obscene, which "the other side" in English only barely suggests.'[10] In this respect, its binary opposite is '*endroit*', connotations of which encompass oppositional directionality—'*droit*' being 'right'—and the politicality of this distinction (that of 'rightwing' in contrast to 'leftwing'); in brief, it might be described as the ostensively seemly side to the seamy side of '*envers*' (where the seams show).

If, as the movie producer Robert Evans famously said, 'there are three sides to every story: your side, my side, and the truth; and no one is lying', this is not only because 'memories shared serve each differently', but gets at Lacan's concept of the 'half-said', in its relation to truth: that—as Lacan puts it—'in short, half-saying is the internal law of every species of enunciation of the truth'.[11] Such is to suggest that the truth is not whole (and nothing but) but, precisely, *not-whole* in itself, structurally: A's rivening, antagonistic position is only partially articulable through positions 1 or 2. Thus, the '*envers*' of enverity lends to this principle an avenue through which we may *observe the obverse*, whilst its 'verity' resides in the very *half-sayableness* that its (divided) structure demands.

To elucidate this structure, we will return to certain examples utilised in—and directly incorporate elements of—the work of *Joyce and Lacan*.

Let us begin with a simple example of the operation of the principle—and its antagonistic structurality—as it is found in the first volume of Karl Marx's *Capital* (of 1867). It is early identified within that work that 'the sale and the purchase [of a commodity] constitute one identical act, an exchange between a commodity-owner and an owner of money, between two persons as opposed to each other as the two poles of a magnet'.[12] Initially, we can see how we are actually met with two derivable models here, the first being that of a commodity and the second of its sale-purchase: so, in the first instance, into position A goes the commodity, into 1 sale, and into 2 purchase; and in the second, into A goes sale-purchase (as 'one identical act'), and into 1 the commodity-owner, and into 2 the money-owner. However, it is the fact that this pronouncement of Marx's draws our attention to the very structurality of 'antagonism' in his system that is of interest here. In the second instance, Marx stresses that the two owners that are involved in the act of a sale-purchase are as opposed as the poles of a magnet. The magnet here holds the place of *antagonism*, in that as well as separating these adversarial poles, it also binds them. This concept of antagonism has its importance further elaborated by Louis Althusser and his students in their reading of Marx, demonstrated by Étienne Balibar's definition given in *Reading Capital* (1968):

> 'Antagonism', 'not in the sense of individual antagonism' (*nicht im individuellen Sinn*), i.e., not a struggle between men but an antagonistic structure; it is *inside the economic base*, typical of a determinate mode of production, and its terms are called 'the level of the productive forces' and 'the relations of production'.[13]

It is an antagonistic structure, *inside the base of things*, that constitutes such an 'identical'—though non-self-identical—act as a commodity's sale/purchase. Thus, the identical act is itself radically antagonistic *in itself*; that is, its structure (or form) is an antagonism which, when sided by its contents—in this case, the buyer (money-owner) and seller (commodity-owner)—becomes apparent; the poles which constitute it are united and separated at once, repellent to one another, but bound, like the poles of a magnet; and a magnet is always structured by its poles: a magnetic monopole is a physical impossibility.

From Marx, let's turn to Freud, and look at the principle's structure in relation to his marginal work 'A Note upon the Mystic Writing-Pad' (1925), in which he refers to and explains the functioning of the familiar toy writing device:

The Mystic Pad is a slab of dark brown resin or wax with a paper edging; over the slab is laid a thin transparent sheet, the top end of which is firmly secured to the slab while its bottom end rests on it without being fixed to it. This transparent sheet is the more interesting part of the little device. It itself consists of two layers, which can be detached from each other, except at their two ends. The upper layer is a transparent piece of celluloid; the lower layer is made of a thin translucent waxed paper. When the apparatus is not in use, the lower surface of the waxed paper adheres lightly to the upper surface of the wax slab.

To make use of the Mystic Pad, one writes upon the celluloid portion of the covering-sheet which rests upon the wax slab[:] a pointed stilus scratches the surface, the depressions upon which constitute the 'writing'. [...] If one wishes to destroy what has been written, all that is necessary is to raise the double covering-sheet from the wax slab by a light pull, starting from the free lower end.[14]

The Mystic Writing-Pad bears a remarkable relation, for Freud, to the systematicity of the psyche. In explaining the doubled property of the transparent sheet in the writing-pad, Freud goes on to say:

If, while the Mystic Pad has writing on it, we cautiously raise the celluloid from the waxed paper, we can see the writing just as clearly on the surface of the latter, and the question may arise of why there should be any necessity for the celluloid portion of the cover. Experiment will then show that the thin paper would be very easily crumpled or torn if one were to write directly upon it with the stilus. The layer of celluloid thus acts as a protective sheath for the paper, to keep off injurious effects from without. The celluloid is a 'protective shield against stimuli'; the layer which actually receives the stimuli is the paper. I may at this point recall that in *Beyond the Pleasure Principle* [...] I showed that the perceptual apparatus of our mind consists of two layers, of an external protective shield against stimuli whose task it is to diminish the strength of excitations coming in, and of a surface behind it which receives the stimuli, namely the system *Pcpt.-Cs.*[15]

To put these reflections back into the terms of the principle of *enverity* we can postulate that behind the 'two layers' of the perceptual apparatus of the mind—the celluloid and paper sheets—(positions 1 and 2), which Freud mentions, lies the unconscious (position A) as their (antagonistically) organisatory principle, that is, *as the wax slab*.

Unconscious

To draw out the 'organisatoriness' of this, we might now re-invoke the chapter entitled 'Front and Back' in literary theorist Pierre Macherey's 1966 work *A Theory of Literary Production*, wherein the words *'endroit'* and *'envers'* are translated variously as 'front', 'outside', and 'back', 'inside', etc., and in which he states: 'the 'front' (*endroit*) and the 'back' (*envers*) can legitimately be regarded as no more than suggestive metaphors. As 'ideas' they are contaminated by the normative fallacy from which they have been only artificially separated.'[16] With the 'normative fallacy' Macherey is exposing the metaphoricity on which these structural *sides*—positions 1 and 2 in the unificatory/separatory principle—rely. Beneath this normative fallacy is position A, a position which it is being revealed through this genealogy might be the only adequate way in which to demonstrate the structurality of certain concepts. Later on, in its place, Macherey identifies his own 'principle of coherence', which unites the front and back, or outside and inside, in a work (of literature). Yet this principle—which Macherey is drawing out here—is not of necessity always one of 'coherence', but it is one which always does *both unite* and *separate* any two 'versions', 'aspects', or *constituents*, of certain structures; a theory which is thus beginning to be uncovered in this passage:

> However you trace the inside (*envers*) and the outside (*endroit*), the work remains unchanged; having been constructed it is stable and continuous. Whether it be actively elaborated or passively followed it offers the same kind of unity, which can be indifferently considered in alternative ways ('in front' and 'behind', to vary our spatial metaphor). Casual appearance or rigorous deduction: these are two versions or aspects of the same reality. The ending unifies them both, and to perceive this unity we relate the work to its necessary conditions. Inside and outside have been only provisionally distinguished in order to demonstrate the principle of coherence in the discourse.[17]

The positions' supposed unity—it is being suggested by Macherey—is due in fact and only to their (coherent) division. Beyond this, with a slight modification, lies the unificatory/separatory principle, which

Macherey is beginning to uncover, but not elaborate on, *as such* (beyond the exposure of the normative fallacy (of the binary) covering over the principle of coherence (of the singularity). Yet this coherence, or unity, is only realisable through its *incoherence*, or division, hence the antagonism that properly undergirds it).

A first clue to the functionality of the enverity principle will be found in a key passage from Ferdinand de Saussure's *Course in General Linguistics* (1906–1911), in which the linguist delineates how we might compare a language

> to a sheet of paper. Thought is one side of the sheet and sound the reverse side. Just as it is impossible to take a pair of scissors and cut one side without at the same time cutting the other, so it is impossible in a language to isolate sound from thought, or thought from sound. To separate the two takes us into either pure psychology or pure phonetics, not linguistics.[18]

Language for Saussure is represented by a piece of paper (position A) on one side of which is thought (position 1), and on the other sound (position 2); and by extension here we can perceive Saussure's linguistic *sign* (A) as a sheet sided by the *signifier* (1) and *signified* (2)—which correspond to the 'sound-image' and 'thought-image' of the sign—and also linguistics as one such sided by psychology and phonetics. This draws our attention again to *l'envers*; the 'other side', or the 'reverse', but also—importantly—to another necessary element in this topology: the sheet. Here unnamed specifically by Saussure, it is that which at the same time *separates* and *unites* these two sides: this founds our principle of *enverity*, or the *unificatory/separatory principle*.

In many ways Saussure's analogy provides a formulation for the unconscious, as it can, too, for structuralism itself. *The sheet*—Saussure's piece of paper—is, then, the structuring principle *without which* we would have neither of its sides, but only *through which* we can have either of them; and yet it is not ontologisable in itself (i.e., without its content it cannot be thought, and with it, it cannot be extricated; that is, it cannot be thought *alone*). In other words, that which *unites* psychology and phonetics in linguistics—and sound and thought in language—is at the same time that which *separates* them from each other; and this sheet that both unites *and* separates can only be thought *abstractly* if without the properties of its sides; that is, it can only be thought purely as *form*, without *content*. It is therefore this very unificatory/separatory principle which such structuralisms as Saussure's linguistics sets out to study, and yet at the same time this principle is taken as their point of departure. As Saussure puts it at the outset of the *Course*: '*the linguist must take the study of linguistic structure as his primary concern*'; setting out from linguistic structure (as a *linguist*) to study linguistic structure (the science of *linguistics*) (this is the 'forward' and 'reverse' implied in Macherey's principle, a pair of contraries that occur at one and the same time).[19]

With this uniting/dividing principle it should be noted that we are not willingly regressing to a reliance on simple binary oppositions, but rather, with it, we are seeking to demarcate certain possible co-dependent originations, hypostases, and inextricabilities that go to make up certain structures, such as the unconscious; that is, structures that might run the risk of being read in a binary way (e.g., the unconscious is a structure in which so many pairings retain great importance, but precisely through their *unity-and-division*, rather than through their binariness, or the symbology of their sides, as it is in the theology-tinged analytical psychology of C. G. Jung). Indeed, contra binarism, we aim to investigate through such *pairing-division* also the *remainder* that gets produced by it; that is, the very sheet which is necessarily present in Saussure's analogy, though it goes unnamed *as such*. Thus, to propose a notion of the unconscious along these lines—which move away from the idea of 'pure' form—we can claim that the unconscious is a sheet sided, for example, by writing (e.g., processes of inscription) and by reading (e.g., the gamut that runs from parapraxes to analysis and interpretation), and that it is its sides' *indivisible remainder*.

As François Regnault—another thinker associated with the structuralist movements of the 1960s in France—precisely puts it, apropos the subject: 'all you need are two signifiers side by side in order to produce the effect of the subject: it is in the interstice of the two, but also disappears there, such that they miss or lack it'.[20] In its linguistic, Saussurian, turn, Lacanian psychoanalytic theory describes a 'signifier [a]s what represents a subject to another signifier'.[21] In his eleventh Seminar, Lacan employs a hieroglyphics analogy 'in order to illustrate this axiom,':

> Suppose that in the desert you find a stone covered with hieroglyphics. You do not doubt for a moment that, behind them, there was a subject who wrote them. But it is an error to believe that each signifier is addressed to you—this is proved by the fact that you cannot understand any of it. On the other hand you define them as signifiers, by the fact that you are sure that each of these signifiers is related to each of the others.[22]

As Regnault puts it, it is in the interstice between signifiers that 'the effect of the subject' is produced; the hieroglyphics on the stone, in Lacan's analogy, of course can only relate one to another via the middle-term of the subject, but *they are addressed one to another*. Co-dependently the subject can only commence decipherment, or inter-pretation, in its very interstice; the interstice of representation between signifiers. And thus—through a slight modification that does not trans-gress this formula's reciprocality—we can even suggest that the subject becomes a *representative*, in something of the ambassadorial sense, for these signifiers. However, Lacan is, too, precisely indicating here that our very status as *subject*—our very *subjectivity*—is the result of *signifi-cation*: of one signifier representing us to another.

We can now array this formula against the three orders that con-stitute Lacan's psychoanalytic system; those of Real, Symbolic, and Imaginary (which are *oscillable* categories, and therefore not fileable into fixed positions in the principle of enverity). The order of the Real for Lacan designates the *impossible* or *unsymbolisable*; one way to think the Real, in relation to the Symbolic, is to read it in terms of trauma: trauma is a close encounter with the Real the first sym-bolic impressions of which we repress; the Real is thus of necessity always foreclosed to—and from—us, and the trauma itself always a 'missed encounter' for us. This is in no way to say that we are not affected by trauma; nothing affects us more. Our connection to it, however, is *discontinuous*, ruptured. The Imaginary effects the impos-sible connection to—or connection-to-the-*impossible* of—trauma, a *disconnection-connection* (*at once*); that is, a *registration* (and repe-tition) of the *missed encounter*. Thus, an explication of Lacan's linguistico-structural formula might run along lines like these: 'we', as *subjects*, are the *remainder* in the Real of our *unity* in the Symbolic and *disunity* in the Imaginary; in other words, the *subject*, the *uncon-scious*, is the (real) *effect* of a signifier's (symbolic) representation to another signifier, and that this effect (the *Real* itself) is overlooked is *effected* by the imaginary, the order which registers *disconnection*, such as from the subject's reflection in the mirror, but *connects* to said mirror-image through this very registration.

In this respect, it is the *unifying division* in structure—*enverity*, or the unificatory/separatory principle—that produces the unconscious and the subject of the unconscious, and thus of psychoanalysis, themselves.

Notes

1 This chapter draws on and adapts work from Daniel Bristow *Joyce and Lacan: Reading, Writing, and Psychoanalysis* (Abingdon: Routledge, 2016).
2 Wilhelm Reich, 'The Interview: 19 October 1952', in *Reich Speaks of Freud* [1967], ed. by Mary Higgins and Chester M. Raphael, trans. by Therese Pol

(Harmondsworth: Pelican Books, 1975) p.87. I have included the symbol—as Figure 1.1—which is displayed in a footnote in the original text.

3 James E. Strick, *Wilhelm Reich, Biologist* (Cambridge, MA: Harvard University Press, 2015) p.10.

4 Ibid.

5 Giordano Bruno, 'Cause, Principle and Unity' [1584], trans. by Robert de Lucca, in *Cause, Principle and Unity, and Essays on Magic*, ed. by Robert de Lucca and Richard J. Blackwell (Cambridge: Cambridge University Press, 1998) p.23.

6 James Joyce, '*L'influenza letteraria universale del rinascimento* [The Universal Literary Influence of the Renaissance]' [1912], trans. by Conor Deane, in *Occasional, Critical, and Political Writing*, ed. by Kevin Barry (Oxford: Oxford World's Classics, 2000) p.188.

7 Sigmund Freud, 'Thoughts for the Times on War and Death' [1915], trans. by E. C. Mayne, in *SE,* XIV, p.296.

8 Ibid.

9 See Sigmund Freud, 'Beyond the Pleasure Principle' [1920], trans. by James Strachey, in *SE*, XVIII, p.39.

10 Russell Grigg, 'Translator's Note', in Jacques Lacan, *The Seminar of Jacques Lacan, Book XVII: The Other Side of Psychoanalysis* [1969–1970], ed. by Jacques-Alain Miller, trans. by Russell Grigg (New York: W.W. Norton, 2007) p.9.

11 Lacan, *Seminar XVII: The Other Side of Psychoanalysis*, p.110; Robert Evans, *The Kid Stays in the Picture* [1994] (London: Faber and Faber, 2004) rev. ed., p.xvii [quotation modified].

12 Karl Marx, 'From Volume One' [1867], trans. by Samuel Moore and Edward Aveling, in *Capital: An Abridged Edition*, ed. by David McLellan (Oxford: Oxford World's Classics, 1995) p.73. I prefer this translation to Fowkes' here because it is more illustrative of the duality inherent in the central concept.

13 Étienne Balibar, 'On the Basic Concepts of Historical Materialism', in Louis Althusser et al., *Reading Capital: The Complete Edition* [1968], trans. by Ben Brewster and David Fernbach (London: Verso, 2015) p.482.

14 Sigmund Freud, 'A Note upon the Mystic Writing-Pad' [1925], trans. by James Strachey, in *SE*, XIX, pp.228–229.

15 Ibid., pp.229–230.

16 Pierre Macherey, *A Theory of Literary Production* [1966], trans. by Geoffrey Wall (Abingdon: Routledge Classics, 2006) p.23.

17 Ibid., p.27.

18 Ferdinand de Saussure, *Course in General Linguistics* [1906–1911], ed. by Charles Bally et al., trans. by Roy Harris (Chicago and La Salle: Open Court, 1986) p.111.

19 Ibid., p.9.

20 François Regnault, 'Structure and Subject' [2009], trans. by Cécile Malaspina, rev. by Peter Hallward, in *Concept and Form: Volume 2, Interviews and Essays on the Cahiers pour l'Analyse*, ed. by Peter Hallward and Knox Peden, 2 vols (London: Verso, 2012) II, p.21.

21 Jacques Lacan, 'The Subversion of the Subject and the Dialectic of Desire in the Freudian Unconscious' [1960], in *Écrits: The First Complete Edition in English* [1966], trans. by Bruce Fink, in collaboration with Hélöise Fink and Russell Grigg (New York: W. W. Norton, 2006) p.695.

22 Jacques Lacan, *The Seminar of Jacques Lacan, Book XI: The Four Fundamental Concepts of Psychoanalysis* [1964], ed. by Jacques-Alain Miller, trans. by Alan Sheridan (New York: W. W. Norton, 1981) p.199.

2 Topology

(Divisions in surface: the Freudian structures)[1]

A cut is another form which enverity can take; it is an operation which unites and separates that which it splits. In an immediate association, 'cut' connects with what we might call the 'obscene underside' of 'coition', or 'coitus'; seemly words connoting 'uniting', as in sexual intercourse. In 1915 the psychoanalyst Viktor Tausk drew attention to the etymology of words that share an affiliation with 'fucking' (*'ficken'*, *'fickeln'*, *'fuxeln'*, *'fugeln'*, etc.); he states: 'words known to mean coitus in obscene speech, in various dialects and speech areas mean cutting or sawing with a blunt instrument'.[2] Thus, that primal scene, which *establishes* the subject, is the *unificatory/separatory* in action: sex, as ever, is at the heart—on the sleeve—of psychoanalysis.

So too is the cut of utmost importance to Lacan, and to the practice of Lacanian psychoanalysis, and in this chapter it will be theorised through developed topological interaction with Lacan's tripartite system of orders, with the aim of presenting more thoroughly the position of the subject (of the unconscious), and this in relation to the clinical psychoanalytic categories—or the 'Freudian structures'—of *neurosis*, hysteric and obsessional; *perversion*; and *psychosis*; and to the role of the symptom, and relation with the object, within each of these.

Topology concerns the study and formulation of *surfaces*, specifically of geometric objects that preserve their precise properties throughout any deformation *that is not a cut* (such as stretching, bending, crumpling, and twisting), and it became the key discipline through which Lacan would formulate his psychoanalytic theory in his late work and final period of teaching. Here, of course, we are concerned with types of cut, and in this chapter we will proceed heuristically towards new definitions and topological modellings through which to figurate cuts, major and minor; positioning the object, and the symptom, within the dialectics of the orders. This will be worked through via two types of

DOI: 10.4324/9781003185239-3

topologisation: Möbial and Borromean (on their possible connection, and derivability from one another, see the appendix to this work).

Through what we will label a 'Möbial topology', we might firstly fathom the Real *as cut*. By contrast, in the Borromean topology that will make up the latter part of this chapter, the Real is cartographed as a ring and/ or infinite line. Heuristic findings from physical experiments made with Möbius strips will be presented here descriptively and diagrammatically (reference to topology textbooks is advised if mathematical formulae are sought).[3]

It is the contention of this section that in the Möbial modelling of the orders—and in accordance with the unificatory/separatory principle—a *third* (in this case, as *cut*) is required to inaugurate any *two*; that is, any binary, or the possibility of distinction at all. Take the simplest Möbius strip: this can most easily be made from a rectangular strip of flexible material (paper, ribbon, etc.), to which is applied a 'half-twist', after which it is joined end-to-end, forming an infinitely linearly traversable surface across a single side; that is, to follow a trajectory lengthwise over the strip will return the navigator to the start-point without the edge being crossed (Figure 2.1).

To conceptualise this structure with no beyond, the indistinction (or what we will later call 'homonomy') of the surface collapses the very possibility of the three orders being distinguished, or distinguishable, at all; there is no *enverity* to this structure, in that what was two-sided unlinked (a sheet of paper with two separate sides, which cannot be cut one from another, and is thus structured by that fact) is single-sided as the Möbius strip (a, properly *real*, amorphousness): in this state, it is a oneness without the horizon of the two. For the horizon of the two to come about, a third element is required: the cut. If we herein figure the cut itself as the Real, it will be through its incisive action that we will arrive at the link of the Imaginary and Symbolic (in the notation of

Figure 2.1 Möbius strip.

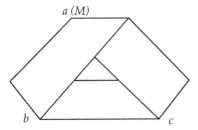

Figure 2.2 Two-dimensional Möbius strip.

the principle of *enverity*, the *cut*, position A, divides the strip into two: positions 1 and 2).

Curious things happen when Möbius strips are cut lengthways. Before tabulating some of these, it will be noted that different results occur should one divide the Möbius strip in half lengthways, or along a third (or other fraction) of its width. Take our simple Möbius strip, which can be depicted flattened out triangularly, or as a hexagon, depicted in two-dimensional representation (Figure 2.2); that is, consisting of three 'flattening-points', as we will call them here (only one of which is *Möbial*—and thus demarcated by (*M*)—and as is elucidated in Figure 2.2). These are the minimal amount of points where the strip crosses over itself when ironed out to be completely flat (*a*, *b*, *c*).

From this simple Möbius strip we will demonstrate what occurs by dividing it lengthways, first along the middle of its width, twice (Example 1), then by splitting it along a third of the width (Example 2).

Example 1

(N.B. All illustrations are not to scale, although the relative sizes are given in the description.)

Description: Cutting the Möbius strip (Figure 2.3: depicted with flattening-points *a* (*M*), *b*, and *c*) in half lengthways (as in Figure 2.4, with cut *x*) creates a single non-Möbial (i.e., two-sided) band (Figure 2.5), double the length and half the width of the original strip (producing a structure with four flattening-points: *d*, *e*, *f*, and *g*). Cutting this in half lengthways again (as in Figure 2.6, with cut *y*) creates two equally sized, directly connected bands (Figure 2.7)—in a Hopf link (i.e., two unknots linked, with two

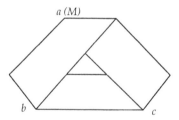

Figure 2.3 Möbius strip.

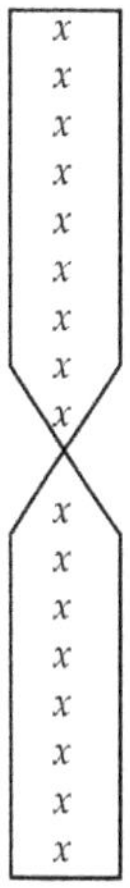

Figure 2.4 Cut x.

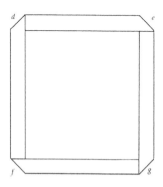

Figure 2.5 Unknot band.

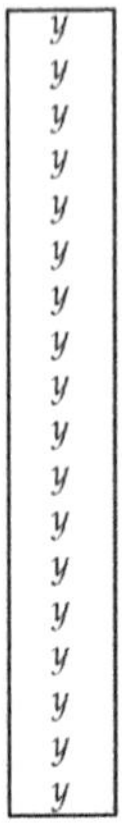

y
y
y
y
y
y
y
y
y
y
y
y
y
y
y
y
y

Figure 2.6 Cut y.

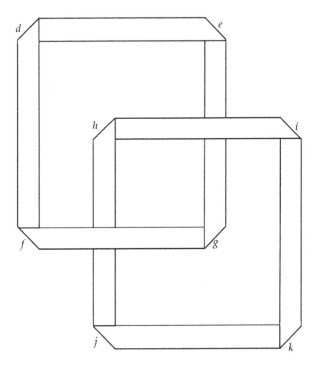

Figure 2.7 Linked unknot bands.

crossing-points)—both of which are now the same length (double that of the original strip) and width (a quarter that of the original strip) as each other. (The second band's flattening-points are demarcated with *h*, *i*, *j*, and *k*).

Example 2

Description: Cutting the Möbius strip (Figure 2.8) along a third of its width (Figure 2.9) ensures the cut loops the strip twice from the point of incision (denoted with cut *x* becoming cut *y* once the point of incision has been passed). This creates a Möbius strip

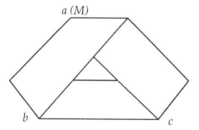

Figure 2.8 Möbius strip.

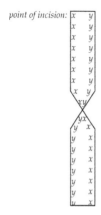

Figure 2.9 Cuts x and y along ⅓ width.

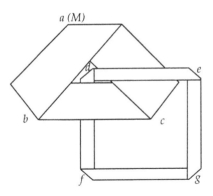

Figure 2.10 Linked Möbius strip and unknot band.

linked to a two-sided band (the same as seen in the first example) (Figure 2.10), the latter double the length of the former, whilst the Möbius strip is two-thirds the width of the original, and the band is one-third the width thereof.

There are other types of Möbius strips—creatable through multiplication of odd-numbered half-twists applied to them—one of which is made from a strip half-twisted thrice and is invoked by Lacan in Seminar XXV, *The Moment to Conclude*, in which—for the purposes of his demonstration—he claims to 'correct' the single half-twist Möbius strip: 'I mean by that to triple it. This is [now] a strip, just like the other, namely, that its front coincides with its back, but this time that happens twice.'[4] This Möbius strip—when ironed out—is depictable again with three flattening points (Figure 2.11), but differently to that of Figure 2.2 (this is because in the once half-twisted strip only one flattening point (*a*) is Möbial, whereas in the thrice half-twisted strip all three are. The thrice half-twisted (or 1.5) Möbius strip is interesting to figure through the halving cut (Example 3) and division along a third of the width (Example 4).

Example 3

(N.B. The cut depictions—designated with *x* and *y*—are the same as in the previous examples and are therefore absent from these.)

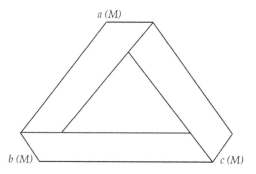

Figure 2.11 1.5 Möbius strip.

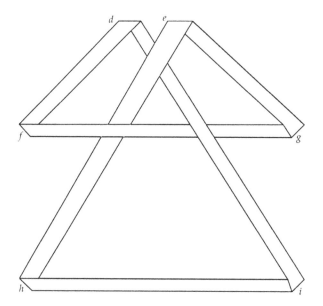

Figure 2.12 Trefoil knot.

Description: Cutting the 1.5 Möbius strip (Figure 2.11; marked with the Möbial flattening-points *a (M)*, *b (M)*, and *c (M)*) in half lengthways produces a two-sided trefoil knot (Figure 2.12), double the length and half the width of the original strip, which

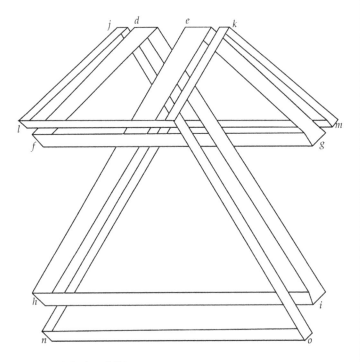

Figure 2.13 Linked trefoil knots.

has six flattening-points (*d*, *e*, *f*, *g*, *h*, and *i*), and three crossing-points, producing its three lobes. Cut in half lengthways again, this creates two linked trefoil knots, of equal size, in a complex knotted structure (Figure 2.13) (the linked trefoil knot's flattening-points are demarcated by *j*, *k*, *l*, *m*, *n*, and *o*).

Example 4

Description: Cutting the 1.5 Möbius strip (Figure 2.14) along a third of its width creates a 1.5 Möbius strip—the same length and two-thirds the width of the original (difficult to depict two dimensionally)—linked with a complicated knotting to a two-sided trefoil knot, twice the length and a third of the original width

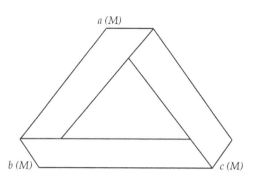

Figure 2.14 1.5 Möbius strip.

(Figure 2.15, page 28). (Interestingly, once the point of incision is reached again, via cutting, on the second circuit of the strip, its trefoil property becomes immediately apparent.)

What these short investigations can figurate in the Lacanian schema is the action of the cut. A major cut coming from the Real to the undifferentiated Möbius strip, we might postulate, divides it into the Imaginary and Symbolic orders—or divides it between the Imaginary and Symbolic registers—both of which are linked in various and differently entangled ways, whilst the Real, as mediator, vanishes again.[5] Whilst these results from experiments with Möbius strips are of interest generally for the RSI triad, and theories of divisions, it is to Lacanian formations of the unconscious and Borromean topology that we will now turn to further explore subjective and unconscious combinations of the orders, and how orders other than the Real can constitute cuts, figured initially through Lacan's schemas and mathemes (from the period popularly formulated as the 'linguistic turn', or what we might call—in homage to Freud—'the first topology') and then as rings and infinite lines (what we could thus call the 'Borromean turn', or 'second topology').

Action: establishing the subject

Lacan—in the *écrit* 'The Instance of the Letter in the Unconscious, or Reason Since Freud' (1957), originally given as an oral presentation—regales his audience with a tale about two children trying to work out

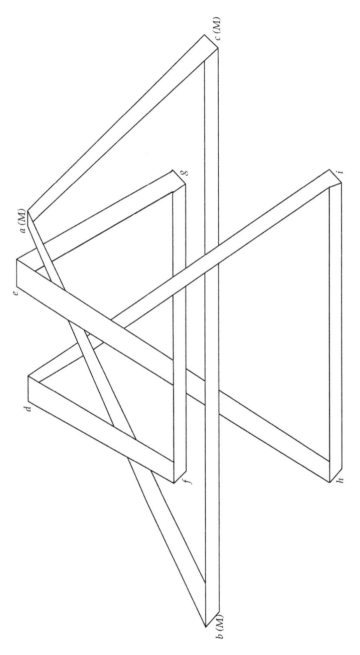

Figure 2.15 Linked 1.5 Möbius strip and trefoil knot.

from two signs that they see at a station whether their train has arrived at the destination 'Ladies' or 'Gentleman', and states that 'the rails in [this] story materialize the bar in the [reversed] Saussurian algorithm' of signifier over signified: $\frac{'S'}{s}$ (a bar which later in his *Écrits* he labels a 'cut').[6]

We could envisage this materialised splitting, or 'schizostructural', bar as the mechanism through which the object cuts into the subject, the object ('*a*') being that which offsets desire, and which in effect is the (*actioning*) equivalent of the (subject of the) unconscious (as *cut*); that is, whilst the object *a* is properly an element of the unconscious—and always and only registered there as missing, *lost*—it is 'put' (or projected) into the Other (broadly, the outside world), to be endlessly searched for there. The equivalency of the subject and object (*a*) is thus unconscious: the object-cause of desire might be redescribed in accord with the shouted commands of a film director as the 'cut-action' of the unconscious—in line with Lacan's statement in 'Position of the Unconscious' (1960), that 'the unconscious is, between the [subject and the Other], their cut in action'—the *cut* of the object spurring on the *action* of the subject. It is this cut into the subject that thereby founds the fundamental fantasy, Lacan's 'mathemetic' formula of which is: '$ ◇ *a*' (barred subject, lozenge, object *a*).

In an extended footnote added in July 1966 to the *Écrits* that summarised his teaching in the *Psychoses* Seminar (III) of 1955–1956—'On a Question Prior to Any Possible Treatment of Psychosis'—Lacan states that he situated the object *a*, in its position in a certain schema that he depicted in the body of the text, 'so as to shed light on what it contributes regarding the field of reality (a field that bars it[; the *a*, that is])'.[7] It is situated in the 'R schema' (Figure 2.16), certain elements of which we will now isolate and investigate:

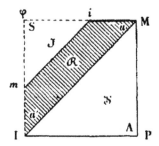

Figure 2.16 The 'R' Schema, based on that in the *Écrits*: 'On a Question Prior to Any Possible Treatment of Psychosis'.

In the footnote, Lacan draws attention to 'the only valid cut in this schema (the cut $\overline{mi}$, $\overline{MI}$)', which delimits the shaded area, R (by following the lines between the positions m and i, and M and I, and joining them up, forming a trapezium, in two dimensions)—and highlights its structure as a Möbius strip (in three dimensions, directionally denoted by the arrows above mi and MI)—containing the object a, and its avatar, a'.[8] Thus, we see that *das Ding* (or 'the Thing'; in effect, the *Ur-object* that is without any cartography) has now boiled down to its compulsive stand-in for the subject, the object a, and its repetitions (a', a'', a''', etc.).

According to Lacan: 'this says it all, since this field [$\overline{mi}$, $\overline{MI}$] will henceforth be the mere placeholder of the fantasy whose entire structure is provided by this cut', by which he means:

Only the cut reveals the structure of the entire surface, because it is able to detach from it the following two heterogeneous elements (noted in my algorithm ($\mathcal{S}\Diamond a$) of fantasy): $\mathcal{S}$—the barred S of the strip to be expected here where it in fact turns up, that is, covering the field R of reality—and a, which corresponds to the fields I and S.

It is thus as representation's representative in fantasy—that is, as the originally repressed—that $\mathcal{S}$, the barred S of desire, props up the field of reality here; and this field is sustained only by the extraction of object a, which nevertheless gives it its frame.[9]

The extraction of object a gives the field of reality—in its disjunction from the Real—its very sustenance (i.e., as the fantasy which covers over the Real, and blocks or bars (access to) the impossible *real* of the object a). As Lacan delineates, it is only the cut that is able to reveal the structure itself, in that it 'detaches' the structure's (two) 'heterogeneous elements' (in this case). That is, whilst linking them, it separates them out too, just like a cut does two scenes in a film. In this respect, the cut again operates along the lines of the *unificatory/separatory principle*, which denotes that which links *and* separates *at once* that which is cut (positions 1 and 2: the Real and reality, or, in the formula of the fantasy, and a), which is brought about, or *actioned, by this cut itself* (position A; the action-cut, or the lozenge in the fantasy formula: '$\Diamond$'). In the instance of the fantasy, it is demonstrable as Figure 2.17.

Thus, the object that originarily founds the fantasy is what Freud designated *das Ding*, which is endlessly attempted to be refound in a succession of objects (a, a', a'', etc.), the attempts at the promotion of which to its status are endlessly made by the subject. Whilst such attempt at promotion is how Lacan formulises sublimation, it also underwrites the functioning of the drive. For example, as he explicates in Seminar IV—in counterpoint to the theories of the Objects Relations

Figure 2.17 Positional demonstration: formula of fantasy.

school of psychoanalysis (the lead exponents of which were Melanie Klein and D. W. Winnicott, and which often took the mother to be the primordial object)—in 'the first Freudian dialectic of the theory of sexuality', it is the 'lack of accord', between what is sought and what is (re)found, in relation to the primordial object, that keeps the drive desirously recirculating (through libidinal stratification, or by alighting on a single stand-in that arrests the fascination and disavows its object-cause (or semblance thereof)—as in the fetish—or through a myriad of other sexual meanderings):

> There is always an essential division, fundamentally conflictual, in the refound object, and by the very fact of its refinding there is always a lack of accord in the object that is refound with regard to the object that is sought. That is the notion with which the first Freudian dialectic of the theory of sexuality is introduced.
>
> This fundamental experience supposes that there is, in the course of the latency period, a conservation of the object in memory, unbe-knownst to the subject, that is to say, a signifying transmission. This object then enters into discord and plays a disturbing role in every later object relation of the subject. It is in this framework, at certain selected junctures and at certain times of evolution, that the strictly imaginary functions are revealed. Everything arising from the pre-genital relation is taken into this parenthesis. Into a dialectic which is first, essentially, in our vocabulary, a dialectic of the symbolic and the real, the imaginary layer is then introduced.[10]

Thus, in terms of the cut *as the unconscious*—and the effects of cuts *as unconscious*, that is, of the unconscious as *the enactment of a cut*, to paraphrase the Lacan of 'Position of the Unconscious' (1960)—the 'signifying transmission' is retained in the memory as the 'conservation of the object'. That which is conserved (of the transmission) is not the object itself *as signified*, but *as signifying*; that is, of course not 'it' in any physical sense, but in the psychical sense, not its *meaning*, but its *address*. Within the primordial framework of relations inaugurated by *das Ding*, in Jean Laplanche's theory of the 'enigmatic signifier', as derived from Lacan, he states that there is 'the possibility that the signifier may be *designified*, or lose what it signifies, without thereby losing its power to signify *to*'—and thus, in extension, it is not only that the signifier may be(come) *designified*, but that it could be primordially *designifiant* (as in the case of *das Ding*).[11] Encounter with *das Ding* is thus a signifying *to*, although enigmatically (i.e., what the signification is *of* proves utterly elusive); so much so is the signification beyond comprehension that only its traces can imaginarily repeat (in a sort of Möbian, or cyclical, manner) in the unconscious and its manifest parapraxes, as endlessly in search of completion in a solid meaning—which will inevitably only elude the grasp of the understanding—as they are. Once this epistemic cut has been instantiated, and its effects become inscribed, its traces symbolically repeat. If this is thus the dialectic of the real and the symbolic that we are articulating, it is the imaginary that (subjectively) connects things up, its functions being revealed in the memorisation of the first symbolic impressions spawned from the real, that have gone on to spur their attempted replication in the emblemata of representation.

What is a major cut may be defined—in Lacan's words in 'The Subversion of the Subject and the Dialectic of Desire in the Freudian Unconscious' (1960)—as one 'made by the signifying chain[, which] is the only cut that verifies the structure of the subject as a discontinuity in the real'.[12] The signifying chain is (an element of) the symbolic, which gets seized upon by the imaginary, by a process of registration (or 'verification'). To return to the R schema; as the cut reveals the structure of the fantasy, covering *over* the real, it thus also verifies the subjective position *in* the real; that is, as a discontinuity within it. That the real is (imaginarily) punctuated by the symbolic allows Lacan—in 'The Situation of Psychoanalysis and the Training of Psychoanalysts in 1956'—to extrapolate from archaeological excavations the assertion that:

> No prehistory allows us to efface the cut brought about by the heteronomy of the symbolic. On the contrary, everything it gives us merely deepens the cut: tools whose serial form directs attention more toward the ritual of their fabrication than toward the uses to which they were put; piles that show nothing other than the symbol anticipating the symbolic's entry into the world; and graves which, beyond any explanation that we can dream up for them, are edifices unknown to nature.[13]

In ruins thus remain runes, the sedimented symbols of the Symbolic. It is due to the Symbolic's 'heteronomy' that symbols can thus (retroactively) anticipate their symbolisation: the Symbolic—its heteronomy—(ostensibly) cuts into the Real, and is connected up by the Imaginary.

A taxonomy of attributes might here be plottable against the three Lacanian orders, if we now phrase things in a topological register derivable from Lacan's pronouncements above: if *heteronomy* defines the Symbolic, then *autonomy* might properly be attributable to the Imaginary (as the realm of the *autos*; that is, of the ego, of the *I*, and of (primary) narcissism: of the *mirage* (*mirror-image*) of (the) self). For the Real we might break, or agglutinate—indeed, both, *at once*, unificatory/ separatorily—this binary with the interjection of *homonomy*, taken here to mean the unnamed/unnameable: the indistinct, undifferentiated, or uncut. Following the above Lacanian (chrono)logic, the process of the three orders' interlinking—and thus also the process of subjectivation itself—can be presented in three stages. (That is, for the purpose of clear diagrammatisation only, we are here dividing a spontaneous phenomenon into sequentiality: a non-temporal, *enverneous* sequentiality). This three-stage process can further be presented in two ways, which will— however provisionally—be labelled 'general' (Figure 2.18) and 'processual' (Figure 2.19):

General:

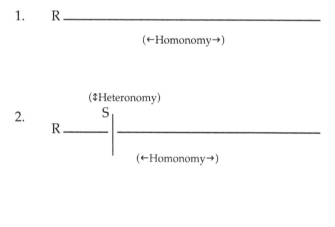

Figure 2.18 'General' homonomy-heteronomy-autonomy schema.

Processual:

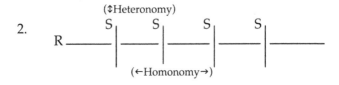

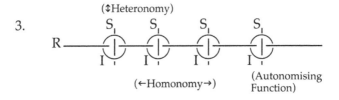

Figure 2.19 'Processual' homonomy-heteronomy-autonomy schema.

To begin with the 'general' presentation:

1   If the Real ('R') is taken as an infinite line, its *homonomy* can be seen as continuous and consistent. We thus depict this here on the horizontal axis.

2   Taken also as an infinite line, the Symbolic ('S') introduces its *heteronomy*, and *appears* to make a cut in the Real. However, this is not actually the case, due to the fact that:

3   The 'autonomising function' of the Imaginary ('I')—its bringing together (unifying) and differentiating (separating) the Real and Symbolic, through its *autonomy*—confirms this tripartite structure as the form known as 'the circle and the cross' (Figure 2.20), which is on the way to depicting a Borromean link (a type of link made of three rings that connects up without any of the rings being directly attached to another):

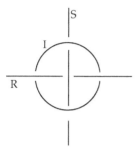

Figure 2.20 The circle and the cross.

This structure is, strictly speaking, only *on the way* to depicting a Borromean link, for—whilst it is true that if any one of its components were to be cut (the ring, or either of the infinite lines), the structure would fully unravel (that is, no two of the other components would remain connected)—whereas the Borromean link has six crossing points, this permutation has only five: four on the circle ('I')—at its intersections with the two axes ('R' and 'S')—and that of the intersection of the two axes of the cross. The vertical and horizontal lines thus need to join end to end respectively, over the existing ring, to themselves become rings (which partake of the property of infinity, in their circularity), which will create the sixth crossing point and therefore the Borromean link.

Thus, whilst the heteronomous process involved in stage 2 initially *appears* to make a cut in the Real, it in fact rather *displaces* the Real, which *brings about* the true cut—that is, the *hole*, at the centre of the Borromean link—only through the third stage; that of the structure's topologisation, enabled by its unificatory/separatory tripartition. This is seeable when given in the structuration of the Borromean link (Figure 2.21):

The 'general' presentation thus gives us the formation of the interlinking of the Real, the Symbolic, and the Imaginary, as three continuous and consistent planes, and as the three constituents of sub-jective psychality; their separateness *from* yet unification *with* each other being the unconscious. If it is this unificatory/separatoriness that is their *cut*, it is the *hole* (formed from the displacements of the orders by their force upon each other) that this cut encircles. As the 'general' presenta-tion, this can be seen to represent the basic situational, or existential, topology of the three orders; constitutive, that is, of the unconscious. The (properly processual) signifying chain itself would in this depiction

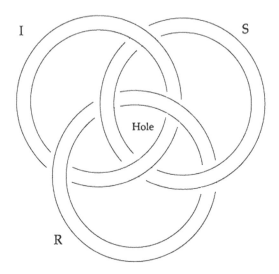

Figure 2.21 Borromean link.

necessitously be inscribed within, or on, the ring of the order of the Symbolic (i.e., if the ring is imagined as a tyre, the chain could then be imagined as its tread, for example).

Thus, the 'processual' presentation separates the signifying chain out into its Symbolic moments or irruptions; into signifiers, that is.

Ergo:

1   The continuous and consistent line of the *homonomy* of the Real ('R') remains the same as in the 'general' presentation at this stage.
2   The Symbolic process of 'signifierisation' (signifiers—that is, 'S's— proliferating) is *heteronomously* introduced.
3   Each is connected up, and thus demonstrated to be separate—that is, *autonomised*—by the Imaginary ('I') function.

If the infinite lines of 'R' and 'S' were again connected end to end in the same manner as above in the 'general' presentation, interesting linkages emerge; that is, the ring of the Real becomes the sustainer of a series of Borromean linkages to it, as such in Figure 2.22.

If the ring of the Real were cut, each of the Imaginary and Symbolic links would come away entirely; however, if one of the Imaginary or Symbolic links were to be cut, it would only effect the dehiscence of

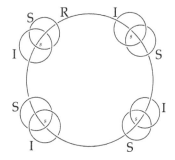

Figure 2.22 'R'-ring with Borromean linkages.

the particularised link of which it is a constituent part (i.e., the dehiscence of the particular *autonomised signifier*). In terms of the 'process'
of the signifying chain, things can thus be apprehended as so: a little bit
of the infinity of real is hooked onto linguistically, whilst the distance
between signifier ('S') and signified (a little bit of real ('*s*'), unsettled
and arbitrary in itself, but established for the time being, in this combinatory signifying process) is maintained by the function of the imaginary.
Each instance is thus the signifierisation ' $\underline{S}$ ', the key to the tablature of
$$\frac{S}{s}$$
which is: 'S' = the signifier (in the Symbolic); '–' = the bar; connector/
divider of the Imaginary (autonomising function); s = the signified, as
an ever-receding little bit of real, unsolidified and constantly (re)fading
as it is approached.

On the infinity of the rings, it becomes clear here that it is only
the Real that is truly infinite, in its homonomy. As symbolised—or
signifierised—as 'bits' of it may become, it still shifts indescribably and
incalculably beneath that process. Thus, linguistically, if—as Saussure
pointed out—'language is differences without positive terms', the Real
is this without differences as well.[14] Likewise, in terms of topographical
placement; as Alexandre Koyré clarifies in *From the Closed World to the
Infinite Universe* (1957):

> The category or question: 'where?' In infinity it has no meaning.
> The infinite is not something, a sphere, of which the center is every-
> where and the limits nowhere; it is something of which the center
> is nowhere also, something that has neither limits nor center, some-
> thing in respect to which the question 'where?' cannot be asked, as
> in respect to it everywhere is nowhere, *nullibi*.[15]

Thus, whatever can become known of the Real—to whatever extent—once it has become so, it is no longer of the Real, but resides in or through the other orders. Therefore, it must also be borne in mind that the topological plane of the Real is only ever—and can only ever be apprehended as—a useful indication, as opposed to anything like a faithful representation. As infinitised, the Real having no 'where' thus implies that at whatever point a signifierisation occurs—at whatever point a signified comes to be established (through a signifier, or what we could call *a* symbolic, imaginarily linking to the Real)—it will strictly be an *arbitrary* point (i.e., in *real* terms).

Re-action: staging the structure

From these introductory remarks, we will work towards a theory of structure—conceptualised on the plane of surface—of the symptom, and its ineradicable counterpart, the *sinthome*, and of *symptom-cutting*. In psychoanalysis, the unconscious is to be taken with the pinch of salt that it rubs into its wound, and this, so often, is the *symptom*. Drawing on the above topological work of the 'general' and 'processual' presentations, we might now set out here a heuristic display of *symptomal topologies*. Doing so is merely intended as a utilisation and theoretical extension of Lacan's late topological work in a fashion that can be utilised and extended, reworked, or completely restructured, in itself; which is to say that it is not to be taken doctrinally or dogmatically, but hopefully productively, clinically and critically. Structurally derived from the foundations of Freud's psychoanalytic theory and method, in Lacanianism there are three prominent psychical (what get inadequately called 'nosographical') categories (the 'Freudian structures', as Lacan referred to them): neurosis, perversion, and psychosis. Within these structures there are also what Freud called 'dialects': hysteria and obsessionality in neurosis, and perhaps what has been extrapolated by Jacques-Alain Miller from Lacan's work on Joyce as the functioning of 'ordinary psychosis', for example. In terms of the symptomal processes involved in these structures, from the schematism of the 'processual' presentation can thus be derived ways of thinking these as links. In so doing, divisions of the Symbolic and Imaginary into discrete elements will be necessitated: those of the signifying chain and its signifiers, in the Symbolic, and the autonomising function(s), and its combinatory signified(s), in the Imaginary, and, in each *individual* instance—that is, in each processual instance of an individual unconscious—the Real should be taken as a ring (whilst this ring is *at the same time* still part of the infinite line of the Real, of course), although it still should be seen as

the key ring, which, if it were to be cut, would dissolve the whole structure, as will be in demonstration throughout.

Initially, we might make the distinction that neurotic (and perverse;
inversely to neurotic) links are 'Borromean' in their properties, whereas
psychotic ones are not (and thus function in another manner, or
might necessitate a form of *sinthomic* 'repair', which will be elucidated
presently).

To set these out: for neurosis, we might depict the hysteric link as in
Figure 2.23 (i.e., as a replica of the third stage of the 'processual' presentation of the homonomy–heteronomy–autonomy intersectionality).

We can highlight here that it is the threading of the Symbolic's
signifiers through the Real and Imaginary that constitutes the neurotic's
signifieds (this will be different in the case of psychosis). In hysteria,
these signifieds thus subsist discretely from one another (as 1, 2, 3, 4, 5,
etc.), and if a signifier were to become hystericised, and thus (its signified
become) symptomatic, it would be this particular symptom-formation
that could be worked on in analysis, and its signifier, or its imaginary
tie, that could be aimed at being cut, to free the symptom from the
linked structure and 'resolve' it. (Another signifier could of course then
be retied to take its place, which could itself then become hystericised,
metonymically, etc. There is no limit to the signifier–signifieds in or on
the link; any quantity would only indicate the 'vocabulary' of the unconscious' structure (which is like a language); a 'vocabulary' which is thus
open to thought processes on the one hand, and symptom-formation
on the other.)

For obsessionality, the weave can perhaps be presented slightly differently, although by still retaining the Borromean property. Instead
of discrete autonomising functions of the Imaginary, we can portray
the Imaginary as a single ring, which holds signifiers (of the Symbolic's
signifying chain) in place against the Real, via a certain weaving, or
braiding (which is to say, if the obsessional signifiers were all to be
under the same weave, they would clump together). Thus, we can show
them as one signifier 'behind' the Real, one 'in front', etc., yet all linked
in Borromean fashion; although this is ultimately dependent, in terms
of crossing-points alone, on which way the Real initially goes to tie into
a ring (which is not the case if it remains infinite). What this means is

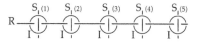

Figure 2.23 Link of hysterical neurosis.

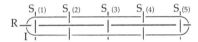

Figure 2.24 Link of obsessional neurosis (the inversion of which is the link of perversion).

that certain signifiers would 'slip off' of the Imaginary if not held in place by others before them.

Take the instances of 1 and 2 in the above diagram of the obsessional link (Figure 2.24). Signifier 2 could not come away of itself from the link, unless 1 had already been removed. Signifier 1 holds 2 in place between itself and 3, but if it were removed, 2 could 'slip off' from the Imaginary via the gap it would have left, whilst 3 'reties' the link, in keeping 4 knotted in between itself and 5 (*ad infinitum*). (This of course also works *in reverse*.) Clinically, obsessionals often display the ability to talk (to 'do the work' of analysis), often of things that would appear quite 'objectively troubling', although these might not be the symptom. That is, there might be a tendency to concentrate on, or *compulsively repeat*, signifier 1, whilst it might in fact be signifier 2 that is at stake, that has become symptomatic. Signifier 1 would then need to be cut to allow signifier 2 to come to the fore, and begin the process of slipping away from the Imaginary. A clinical example might take the form of an analysand whose compulsive behaviour away from analysis involves an addiction-like repetition of an inhibiting action (say, online gambling; inhibitive perhaps of money accumulation, or social interaction beyond the computer and the digital green felt of poker and roulette table graphics). However, in analysis the obsessional might find themselves unable to talk about this, and thus talk instead about (what they may consider to be the *expected*) tropes of Oedipal relations; 'daddy–mummy–me', as Gilles Deleuze and Félix Guattari have it, etc. However, relations to—or between—these Oedipal players might one day change (say, if someone in the Oedipal triad is stricken with a grave illness); this perhaps in itself may cut that signifier—or ready it to be cut in the analysis (it might resonate with something in it: death, perhaps; a favourite theme of the obsessional)—freeing up the signifier 'behind' it, symptomatic of the compulsive behaviour. As a cut in the life of the analysand, this process might be phrased by them as: 'in relation to this major event, my symptom seems smaller-scale, and therefore I can bring it up now (that is, under this pretence).' (What is unavoidably implied in this topologisation is a sequentialisation of signifiers/symptoms, which of course proves problematic, but perhaps also representative of the problematics the treatment of obsessionality can face. What this sequentialisation thus seems to imply is that it might be more than one 'barring' signifier that needs to be worked on to free up a symptom— and, necessarily, other (perhaps non-symptomatic) signifiers, in the 'vocabulary'—to be able to assume the position of 'detachability'. We could however envisage along the line of the Real discrete 'clumps' of numerous signifiers held in place by separate (autonomising) Imaginary rings, for example.) What thus links the neurotic structures, in this theorisation, is their *Borromeanicity*, yet it is the particular manifestation of this that separates them from each other.

In the *Three Essays on the Theory of Sexuality* (1905), Freud put forward the thesis that *'neurosis is, so to speak, the negative of perversion'*.[16] However, this is in no way incompatible with Lacan's identifying perversion as a purely different structure to neurosis. It is. Yet it is also a structure which can be presented as partaking of the Borromean property. Indeed, as Dylan Evans helpfully elucidates:

> Freud's remark that 'the neuroses are the negative of the perversions' has sometimes been interpreted as meaning that perversion is simply the direct expression of a natural instinct which is repressed in [neurosis]. However, Lacan rejects this interpretation entirely (S4, 113, 250). Firstly, the drive is not to be conceived of as a natural instinct which could be discharged in a direct way; it has no zero degree of satisfaction. Secondly, as is clear from the above remarks, the pervert's relation to the drive is just as complex and elaborated as that of the neurotic. From the point of view of genetic development, perversion is at the same level as neurosis; both have reached the third 'time' of the Oedipus complex (S4, 251). Perversion therefore 'presents the same dimensional richness as [a neurosis], the same abundance, the same rhythms, the same stages' (S4, 113). It is therefore necessary to interpret Freud's remark in another way: perversion is structured in an inverse way to neurosis, but is equally structured (S4, 251).[17]

Thus, for comprehending perversion's structure against the above neurotic links, we can likely come closest to it if we were to swap the role of the signifiers of the Symbolic ('S's) with that of the Imaginary loop ('I') in the obsessional neurotic presentation (in Figure 2.24), thus arriving at the inverse of that structure. Evans suggests—drawing on and condensing a schema of Lacan's in the *écrit*, 'Kant with Sade'— that if the formula for (neurotic) fantasy is '$\$ \diamond a$', for perversion it becomes '$a \diamondsuit \$$'; that is, fantasy's inverse.[18] This is because the pervert locates themselves—imaginarily—as locus of the Other's enjoyment, or as the object through which the Other enjoys. In other words, in perversion the object a is identified with, not sought; its being sought—by the Other, 'A' (which gets diluted into *others*; other people: '$\$$'s)—is the 'turn-on', so to speak, and to (attempt to) fulfil the Other's desire (*completely*, at whatever symbolically destituting cost) the goal. Thus, as an inversion of neurotic fantasy, the moment of identification (of the imaginary) in perversion is with the a (which, as a notation, doesn't need barring—like the upper case 'A' of the big Other—as it is constitutively barred in its very structurality, as an always already missing or lost object; which is why the upper case 'A' does get barred, in its *ex-plicit* reflection of this quality in the a). It is in the barred Other ('$\bar{A}$') that the pervert searches for a gap to fill; that is, what are seen as cuts in the Symbolic Other—or, to use the schematic notation: as '/'s (which bar 'A' as '$\bar{A}$')—the pervert tries to imaginarily stop up, *as a*; that is, to complete (the jouissance, or 'enjoyment', of) the Symbolic (as *jouis-sens*, or 'enjoy-meant'). Thus, whereas in the obsessional link, the symptomal signifieds are made up of individual symbolic signifiers being imaginarily linked to the real, in the perverse link, it is through individual imaginary identifications that the signifieds are produced. That is, $S_{(1)}$, $S_{(2)}$, etc., would get replaced with $I(a)_{(1)}$, $I(a)_{(2)}$, etc., which stand for so many positions (1, 2, 3...) of the object a that get identified with by discrete functors of the Imaginary (its autonomising functions; though objectally directed in this instance, as opposed to subjectively, as in the hysteric's link).

Yet, in the perversion formula derived from Lacan, it seems that the sights are set on the position of the barred subject; that is, *from* the a ($\$$ being what lies beyond the lozenge's 'desire for', as Lacan labels it in 'Kant with Sade').[19] That is, there seems here to be an unconscious idea that a form of subjectivity is arrivable at in the full realisation of (one's) objectality. If for the neurotic subject its enframing subtraction from (and thus insertion into) reality (fantasmatically) positions it as a *hole*, in search of its object a, for the pervert (or, more strictly, in the inverted fantasy of perversion), *as* the a, it is the *hole* that is sought (even if disavowedly; as in fetishism, which Lacan called the 'perversion of perversions'[20]). Thus, to further the above, in the inversion of the obsessional link, it is discrete moments of the Imaginary—*identifications*—that are linked by the Symbolic loop to the Real, forming the signifieds of perversion, and it is thus these moments of identification that can become symptomatic, liable to result in actings-out, or more consequential *passages à l'acte*; enactings of the object a, although ones in which the assumed mediation, or commands, of the Other may have become skewed in the pervert's purview.

In Seminar X, Lacan gives the example of Freud's case of a young homosexual woman—identified as one pertaining to the perverse structure—in which, in 'fling[ing] herself, *niederkommt*, let[ting] herself drop' onto a railway track, in a botched suicide attempt, she 'is brought into relation with what [s]he is as *a*', due to an impasse that does not allow her reaction to a sudden traumatic manifestation to be neurotically symbolised; that is, to take the form of a *linguistic* symptom.[21] Thus, it can be suggested that in the neurotic, the symbolic's passage to the real is via the imaginary; in the pervert, it is the imaginary that attempts to make a passage to the real, via the symbolic. If the symbolic is the mediator in the latter instance, then it is through it that the imaginary must pass; the symbolic thus takes on the attribute of an *outside* language—as opposed to the private language of a neurotic, which they attempt to make understood to or by the outside—into which an act, an object, can be written: the *falling* of a woman considered *fallen*.

It might be remarked that whilst a linguistic structure always underwrites the unconscious, its symptomal manifestations range between the Freudian psychical categories. Thus, in neurosis symptoms manifest most prominently in language as it is thought and spoken (therefore, as the very stuff of the classical 'talking cure'); that is, as disturbances of the symbolic. In perversion, they manifest most prominently in acts—often *beyond the social* (i.e., the symbolically strictured and structured; whether in statuted law, or morality *à la mode*)—in reaction-formation to *unsymbolisablity*; that is, when an *impasse* of symbolisation creates a *passage* to the (bodily) act. These may thus be construed as disturbances of the imaginary (considered the locus of the body, from the mirror-stage, and its misrecognitions, onwards).

In psychosis, it is perception that is affected symptomally. In terms of the topologies attributed to psychosis (by Lacan himself, and others), this is due to faults in the (*percipiens*') tie to *percepti*, and in the structure of the *percepti* themselves, within the psychotic link. That is, generally, what is perceived (*percepti*) is made up of the Real and Symbolic, and tied to (in the phenomenon of perception) by the Imaginary (of the *percipiens*, or the perceiving subject). In psychosis, however, it appears that the Real and Symbolic are directly tied together (not connected only through the Imaginary, as in a Borromean link), and the Imaginary insufficiently connected to them, in one way or another. That is, when describing a psychical structure derived from his knowledge of the work and life of James Joyce in Seminar XXIII—known as *The*

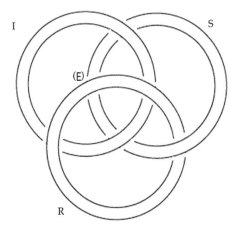

Figure 2.25 Imaginary 'wedged' between linked Symbolic and Real.

Sinthome—Lacan formulates a link in which, with Real and Symbolic directly tied, the Imaginary is 'wedged' between them (Figure 2.25):[22]

As can be seen, the Symbolic ring ('S') threads directly through that of the Real ('R'), the Imaginary ('I') being held in place between these two. This formulation of 'Joyce's link' has since led to the designation of the functioning of 'ordinary psychosis', which, because the Imaginary is maintained in its position, unless an excess of pressure is applied to it, can typically present as a neurotic structure (or as its inverse), until a rupture (in which the escape of the bodily—and its perception—from the subject of this structure might be discerned). (Thus, prior to any rupture, the link may be misrecognised as Borromean, whilst it is in fact not.) To 'rectify' this possibility inherent in this link, a *sinthome* (a utilisable fundament of the undissolvable symptom) can be tied around the rings of the Real and Symbolic in the space demarcated '(E)' above—that is, that awaiting the *sinthome* (the siglum for which was chosen from Joyce's last major work *Finnegans Wake* (1939) in my previous work on Joyce and Lacan)—by weaving a ring from point '(E)' under the Symbolic, over the Real, back under the Symbolic, and again over the Real, and connecting it up as a full ring back at point '(E)', as in Figure 2.26.

To the function of the *sinthome* we will return after elucidating the last of the symptomal links that will here feature, that of psychosis (which is also repairable in a *sinthomic* fashion, although more fragilely). Lacan does not give a topology of psychosis in his late work (nor

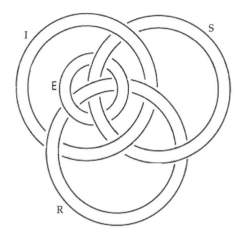

Figure 2.26 The *sinthome* repairing link of Figure 2.25.

does he identify the Joycean structure as psychotic), but one fashioning of its possible construction is extrapolated by Raul Moncayo in his reading companion to Seminar XXIII, in which the Imaginary, instead of being wedged between the linked Symbolic and Real, is completely separate to them, 'resting' on top of or underneath these linked rings.[23] A specially threaded *sinthome* is then able to tie the Imaginary ring back to the others. Prior to this, however, the Imaginary is in a sense out on its own, sometimes touching the linked Symbolic and Real, but not properly linking to them, and thus receiving what could be termed their echoes and mirages; thus *perceiving their influence*, to use Tausk's term. Moncayo's links—of, in his words, 'three psychosis' ('R', 'S', 'I') and 'four psychosis' (the three, retied with the *sinthome*: 'E'), brought in line with the ordering of the above Joycean links—are thus those of Figures 2.27 and 2.28.

In this, the Imaginary 'rests' up against two points on the Symbolic and one on the Real, although it is in no way secured to these orders. With the ring of the *sinthome* fixed in place, a securement occurs, stabilising psychotic perception to an extent (although the Imaginary's room for wayward manoeuvre is not as constrained as in the link of 'ordinary psychosis' tied by the *sinthome*).

To return to symptoms and *sinthomes*: a clinical example of a psychotic symptom may be seen in an analysand who, in their speech, returns to an instance in their youth in which they had violently attacked a parent. They now hear voices, which are described as giving them a

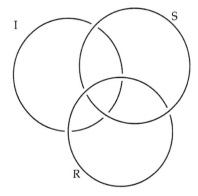

Figure 2.27 Link of 'three psychosis'.

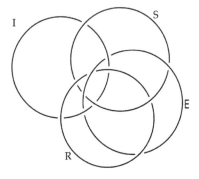

Figure 2.28 Link of 'four psychosis'.

good hiding every now and then. In this physical attribution to the voices of bodily attacking the analysand represents a displacement of the earlier event, through a metaphor that manifests itself in the perception (in itself displacing the linguistic structure of the unconscious into its reappearance in the system of perception). In the structure of this psychotic symptom, a direct relation is foreclosed due to the fact that the Imaginary does not and cannot thread—or wedge itself—between the Symbolic and Real (i.e., the symbolic is taken to be the real; it is perceived as such: *as* an actual 'hiding', not as the signifier 'hiding', from which its associations can propel interpretation and overdetermination. The signifier is thus literally hidden here; foreclosed).

However, the symbolic, and its signifying chain, can be modified in these versions of psychosis by the introduction of the *sinthome*. Thus, whilst it is not the signifier that founds the psychotic symptom (in this presentation of things), it could be deployed in various ways to adjust the psychotic experience. Thus, to adapt Moncayo's links to the plane of the signifying chain, we can show three symptomal stages of psychosis (Figures 2.29–2.31):

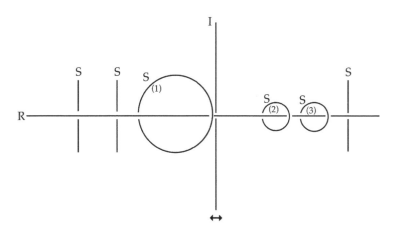

Figure 2.29 Link of psychosis on signifying plane.

Thus, here we see the Real ('R') and Imaginary ('I') as infinite lines, and the Symbolic ('S') broken down into the signifying chain, between two signifiers of which (1 and 2; directly linked to the Real, as they are) the Imaginary finds itself (perhaps correlative to the two points of the Symbolic on which the Imaginary was seen to 'rest' above); its vacillation between these points—and in general (as it is untied to the linked Real and Symbolic)—is demarcated by the arrows. After the third signifier (unavailable to the Imaginary currently) the other signifiers of the chain are foreclosed and cannot be apprehended.

2

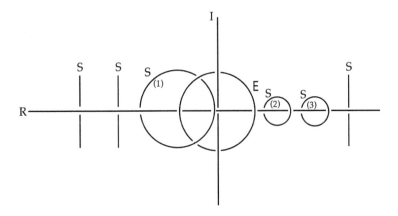

Figure 2.30 Link of psychosis on signifying plane, with *sinthome*.

With the *sinthome* ('E') applied, the Imaginary gets tied in place, and is unable to escape the structure. It can no longer move as much between signifiers, although it has been given the safety net of the *sinthome* so that it does not simply slip away. 'S$_{(2)}$', however, has become temporarily out of its reach—the others still foreclosed—until the next stage.

3

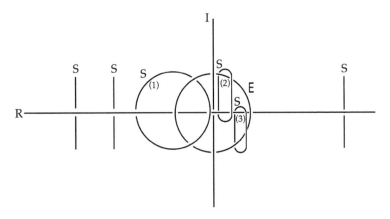

Figure 2.31 Link of psychosis on signifying plane, with extended *sinthome*.

In this third stage, the signifiers that might be available to the psychotic Imaginary can be linked to by extension of the *sinthome*; that is, to thread through 'S$_{(2)}$' and 'S$_{(3)}$', which previously wasn't available at all. These extra signifiers can thus hold the Imaginary more securely in place, whilst the others in the chain necessitously remain foreclosed, as per the structure; the non-Borromean structure of psychosis, that is. To couch this in clinical terms; if, classically, a signifier represents a subject to or for another signifier, in psychosis the subject seems to find themselves outside of this exchange. According to the above schemas, the psychotic imaginary has assumed the place of a signifier, occupying its position in the signifying chain, as if it were on the conveyor belt of language, the movement of which being completely beyond its control, beyond the reach of its autonomising function; that is, the imaginary here is utterly interpellated, and thus perceives the symbolic *as real*. Its sliding proximity to the two signifiers at its disposal puts their significations into the realm of perception; as hallucinations, for example. They are not connected to and separated from at once (in the manoeuvre of the unificatory/separatory principle) imaginarily, as occurs in the neuroses, and inversely in perverse identifications, but metastasise in various distortions of reality (brought about by a different—closer perhaps—relation to the real). In psychosis, meaning might *shine*; it might be transmitted by rays. The likelihood of the establishment of a transference in its analysis is diminished in that for psychosis *everything* might well already (be perceived to) *be* transference.

If we very simply imagine the Imaginary of the neuroses and perversion as a horizontal axis, and that of the psychoses as a vertical one, we can picture the imaginaries of analyst and analysand as 1) linking (neurotic/pervert—neurotic/pervert), and signifiers being put in exchange between them, but in the meeting of analyst and analysand when the psychoses are involved, imaginaries not connecting, but 2) intersecting (neurotic/pervert—psychotic), or 3) running parallel (psychotic—psychotic); that is, as:

1) — —
2) — |
3) | |

The fourth relation—psychotic—neurotic/pervert: '| —'—(as well as the third) may have been what Lacan saw himself as ending up operating in his clinic, in identifying as psychotic himself in his late stages.[24] The cuts that this analytic setup provoked could often be radical, as attestations of Lacan's late clinic bear out.[25]

What might be aimed at, then, in analysis of psychosis, is the sliding of signifiers towards the imaginary to fasten it in place more securely.

Thus, in the treatment of its 'raw' state (versions of which—paranoia, schizophrenia, etc.—are omitted here), the imaginary's connection to the symbolic could be concentrated on, with its realisation as symbolic (i.e., as not overwhelmingly *real*) as the goal thereof. This could perhaps be presented as the closing-in around the imaginary of '$S_{(1)}$' and '$S_{(2)}$' in stage 1 above (of course with an emphasis on the supportiveness of the closing-in, as opposed to its being taken in a persecutory sense). The establishment of a *sinthome*—which could be aimed at in analysis, through the *assumption* of the irreducible aspect of a symptom, as Lacan phrases it in his late work—would prevent the imaginary escaping (which might typically manifest in some form or other of an 'episode'), as seen in the second stage. In the third; in the treatment, the imaginary might be further buttressed by weaving the *sinthome* onward through the next two signifiers linked to the real ('$S_{(2)}$' and '$S_{(3)}$'), to secure the imaginary at two further points. In this structure, this thus seems to be the ultimate result of the last re-sort.

Finally, to return to the Joycean structure of psychality; ordinarily, with the imaginary wedged in place, symptoms typical of the neurotic structure might present; that is, until some pressure forces a dehiscence of the imaginary, which the treatment could work on re-wedging. However, if the structure's *sinthomic* repair has been carried out (with(in) or without analysis; Joyce's was certainly of the latter, as Lacan is constantly at pains to remind us) then something new can occur with signifiers, in the realm of creation, or *creative writing*; that is, the signifier can come to *stuff the signified*, as Lacan said of Joyce's compositional practice in Seminar XX.[26] This can thus be presented (as Figure 2.32):

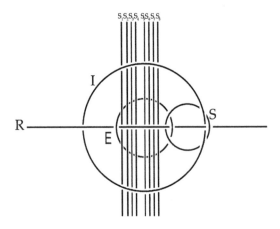

Figure 2.32 'Joyce's link'.

Here, it is as if signifiers themselves have broken loose of the signifying chain. Whilst the Symbolic order ('S') is still directly linked to the Real ('R'), signifiers ('S$_1$', 'S$_2$', 'S$_3$', etc.) are now able to thread through the reattached Imaginary ('I') and the *sinthome* ('E'), which function in conjunction as the place of the signified (stuffed with the signifier). Whilst signification thus abounds, the risk of its overloading the subject seems to have been countered by the securement enabled by the *sinthome*; that is, there can be a push in this particular linking made towards taking signification as far as it can go, cranking up its level of tension and intensity, its *intension*—to and perhaps beyond infinity, as the signifiers' presentation as infinite lines here suggests—whilst the Symbolic remains grounded, separating this adventure of sense from madness. (It is as if the end of a language might have been reached, and its beyond thus become explorable; Joyce indeed said that he had taken English as far as it could go with *Ulysses* (1922), the beyond of which was *Finnegans Wake*.[27] In Stanley Kubrick's *2001: A Space Odyssey* (1968), the Stargate conducts a similar reaching-beyond of subjectivity, carried out in the film on the visual and spatio-temporal plane).

Cut: calling time

With these presentations of links pertaining to the Freudian structures (in which untyings and retyings of themselves might always be taking place), we are enabled to envisage different ways in which, and means by which, symptoms can be cut, modulated, or sutured (in this last instance with the *sinthome*, which can come about through the *assumption* of a symptom—that is, connecting to the symptom's *real*—locatable for instance in the *assumption*, or accepting-as-true, of one's structure as psychotic, at any one time, from which sutural work with signifiers might commence). Specifically in terms of *symptom-cutting*, we might postulate that in the structures of neurosis, in which signifiers *flare* into symptoms, and that of perversion, in which certain identifications (with objects *a*) can become symptomatically dangerous or unhealthily detrimental to the analysand, their cuts can come about in analytic treatment through its cuts, major and minor: interpretations, silences, scansions, moments of concluding, highlightings of the holes in the analytic dialectic's discourse.

Retrospectively, these cuts may be seen as major or minor according to whether they had brought about a symptom's resolution or dissolution, or whether they had modified or modulated it in the direction of these results (obviously, if a cut had been attempted in the service of these results with neither achieved, it cannot be said to be either minor

or major, and if a cut were made with inverse, unintended effects—
unexpected retrogressions, triggerings, episodes, or outbreaks—they
too could be adversely minor or major).

One practical method of cutting—that could result in either (or neither) of these results—that Lacan employed was the variable-length
analytic session. In 'The Function and Field of Speech and Language
in Psychoanalysis' (1953), Lacan broaches this subject, turning to discussion of the length of sessions.

> Here again it is a question of an element that manifestly belongs to
> reality, since it represents our work time, and viewed from this angle
> it falls within the purview of professional regulations that may be
> considered predominant.
>
> But its subjective impact is no less important—and, first of all,
> on the analyst. The taboo surrounding recent discussion of this
> element is sufficient proof that the analytic group's subjectivity is
> hardly liberated on this question; and the scrupulous, not to say
> obsessive, character that observing a standard takes on for some if
> not most analysts—a standard whose historical and geographical
> variations nevertheless seem to bother no one—is a clear sign of the
> existence of a problem that analysts are reluctant to broach because
> they realize to what extent it would entail questioning the analyst's
> function.[28]

What he is highlighting here is the somewhat arbitrary—or *geo-
historically determined*—setting of the length of sessions at the '50-
minute hour' mark (which does not correspond to the '*enverneous*'
timelessness of the unconscious). Cutting the session earlier (this
happened *in extremis* in Lacan's late clinical practice)—or even
lengthening its moment to conclude beyond the standardised time
(which happened far less, and to the idea of which Lacan was less
inclined; although Winnicott would often operate in this way, for
example)—could enable something to occur at a precise point, which
the analysand could 'take away' with them. This not only includes a
cut leaving the analysand with a certain signifier on which to ruminate,
it could also entail a challenge being made to an analysand's mode of
discourse, for example. That is to say, if the cut came suddenly, during
a flabby moment of repetitious literary criticism conducted from the
couch—as is Lacan's example in 'The Function and Field'—over the
time between sessions this could be reflected on and questioned, and in
the next session something more subjectively substantive might become
the topic that speech alights on, which might not have been talked about

otherwise.[29] Further, in anticipating the end of a session, an analysand has (a certain) time to prepare, perhaps by constructing a finale, conclusion, or summative statement which ties everything together (a bit too) neatly, or by watching the clock, specifically so as to put the blame on it when time runs out that there was not enough time to get to the point, or to cover everything. Thus, Lacan states:

> The ending of a session cannot but be experienced by the subject as a punctuation of his progress. We know how he calculates the moment of its arrival in order to tie it to his own timetable, or even to his evasive maneuvers, and how he anticipates it by weighing it like a weapon and watching out for it as he would for a place of shelter.[30]

Indeed, it can be on the punctuation of an analytic session's scansion that so much can come to rest, for as Lacan says: 'punctuation, once inserted, establishes the meaning; changing the punctuation renews or upsets it; and incorrect punctuation distorts it.'[31] These risks taken in the dialectic of analysis are those that might determine whether or not a symptom will be given (new) meaning, or become further upset, or be distorted; the punctuation of its cuts might indeed have minor or major effects, re- or defamiliarising effects; and might become the moment in which the dehiscence of a troubled signifier or identification might be effected. In the operation of these cuts, the surfaces of space and time distort, phenomena unite and separate, and the holes of discourse are drawn attention to.

Notes

1 This section is an adaption of the chapter entitled 'Cut', in Daniel Bristow, *2001: A Space Odyssey and Lacanian Psychoanalytic Theory* (Cham: Palgrave, 2017).

2 Viktor Tausk, 'On the Psychology of the Alcoholic Occupation Delirium' [1915], trans, by Eric Mosbacher and Marius Tausk, in *Sexuality, War and Schizophrenia: Collected Psychoanalytic Papers*, ed. by Paul Roazen (Abingdon: Routledge, 2017) p.116, n.4. Tausk was drawing on a study by Hanns Sperber.

3 Recommended introductory works would be Stephen Barr, *Experiments in Topology* [1964] (New York: Dover, 1989); Bert Mendelson, *Introduction to Topology* [1962] (New York: Dover, 1990); and Wilson A. Sutherland, *Introduction to Metric and Topological Spaces* (Oxford: Oxford University Press, 2009). In an earlier version of this chapter, the cross-cap is discussed,

and beyond that in the book, the Klein bottle. See Bristow, *2001: A Space Odyssey and Lacanian Psychoanalytic Theory*.

4   Jacques Lacan, *The Seminar of Jacques Lacan, Book XXV: The Moment to Conclude* [1977–1978], trans. by Cormac Gallagher (Unofficial translation, n.d.) session 10, 11 April 1978, p.1.

5   The *undifferentiality* could be a metaphorical reason to give for the surface's mathematical non-orientability, to stretch the terminology.

6   Jacques Lacan, 'The Instance of the Letter in the Unconscious, or Reason Since Freud' [1957], in *Écrits*, p.417.

7   Jacques Lacan, 'On a Question Prior to Any Possible Treatment of Psychosis' [1955–1956], in *Écrits*, p.486, note 14. The R schema is depicted on p.462.

8   Ibid.

9   Ibid., pp.486–487, n.14.

10 Jacques Lacan, *The Seminar of Jacques Lacan, Book IV: The Object Relation, 1956–1957*, ed. by Jacques-Alain Miller, trans. by L. V. A. Roche (Unofficial translation, n.d.) p.50.

11 Jean Laplanche, *New Directions for Psychoanalysis* [1987], trans. by David Macey (Oxford: Basil Blackwell, 1989) p.45.

12 Lacan, 'The Subversion of the Subject', in *Écrits*, p.678.

13 Jacques Lacan, 'The Situation of Psychoanalysis and the Training of Psychoanalysts in 1956', in *Écrits*, p.392.

14 See Ferdinand de Saussure, *Course in General Linguistics* [1906–1911], ed. by Charles Bally et al., trans. by Wade Baskin (Glasgow: Fontana/Collins, 1974) rev. ed., p.120.

15 Alexandre Koyré, *From the Closed World to the Infinite Universe* [1957] (Baltimore: The Johns Hopkins University Press, 1968) p.201. The concept of 'nullibiety'—that Lacan draws on in the 'Seminar on 'The Purloined Letter''—finds especial resonance in relation to topological space; indeed, the above-described property of the Möbius strip's indistinction and amorphosity (conceptualised with *no beyond*) can be read as partaking of the *everywhere-and-nowhere-at-once* that Koyré's *nullibi* points to. See Jacques Lacan, 'Seminar on "The Purloined Letter"' [1956], in *Écrits*, p.16.

16 Sigmund Freud, *Three Essays on the Theory of Sexuality: The 1905 Edition*, ed. by Philippe van Haute and Herman Westerink, trans. by Ulrike Kistner (London: Verso, 2016) p.26.

17 Dylan Evans, *An Introductory Dictionary of Lacanian Psychoanalysis* (London: Routledge, 1996) p.142. To Evans' references to the French of Seminar IV, compare Lacan, *Seminar IV: The Object Relation*, pp.113–114 and pp.289–290.

18 See Evans, *An Introductory Dictionary of Lacanian Psychoanalysis*, p.142, in which he refers to Jacques Lacan, 'Kant with Sade' [1963], in *Écrits*, p.653.

19 See ibid.

20 Lacan, *Seminar IV: The Object Relation*, p.223.

21 Jacques Lacan, *The Seminar of Jacques Lacan, Book X: Anxiety* [1962–1963], ed. by Jacques-Alain Miller, trans. by A. R. Price (Cambridge: Polity, 2014) p.110.

22 See Jacques Lacan, *The Seminar of Jacques Lacan, Book XXIII: The Sinthome*, ed. by Jacques-Alain Miller, trans. by Adrian Price (Cambridge: Polity, 2016) p.130.

23 See Raul Moncayo, *Lalangue, Sinthome, Jouissance, and Nomination: A Reading Companion and Commentary on Lacan's Seminar XXIII on the Sinthome* (London: Karnac, 2016) pp.v–viii. Moncayo's extrapolation of a link of neurosis (depicted as three unconnected—and thus desubjectivated—rings), however, is contrary to its workings in Seminar XXIII, and completely unsustainable subjectively.

24 On this, for example, see Stijn Vanheule, *The Subject of Psychosis: A Lacanian Perspective* (Basingstoke: Palgrave Macmillan, 2011) p.163.

25 See, for example, the chapter 'Psychoanalysis Reduced to Zero', in Elisabeth Roudinesco, *Jacques Lacan: An Outline of a Life and a History of a System of Thought* [1993], trans. by Barbara Bray (Cambridge: Polity Press, 1999) pp.385–398.

26 Jacques Lacan, *The Seminar of Jacques Lacan, Book XX: Encore: On Feminine Sexuality, the Limits of Love and Knowledge, 1972–1973*, ed. by Jacques-Alain Miller, trans. by Bruce Fink (New York: W. W. Norton, 1998) p.37.

27 Joyce is claimed to have remarked, in French: '*Je suis au bout de l'anglais* ['I'm at the end of English'], [...] to August Suter, and [...] to another friend, 'I have put the language to sleep.'' See Richard Ellmann, *James Joyce: New and Revised Edition* (Oxford: Oxford University Press, 1983) p.546.

28 Lacan, 'The Function and Field of Speech and Language in Psychoanalysis [1953]', in *Écrits*, p.257.

29 See Lacan, ibid., p.259: 'In experimenting with what have been called my "short sessions," at a stage in my career that is now over [...] I was able to bring to light in a certain male subject fantasies of anal pregnancy, as well as a dream of its resolution by Cesarean section, in a time frame in which I would normally still have been listening to his speculations on Dostoyevsky's artistry.'

30 Ibid., p.258.

31 Ibid.

3 Enverneity
(Divisions in temporality: outside-time)[1]

Time out-of-joint: enverneity

Lacan begins his last Seminar—before its dissolution—*Topology and Time* (1978), with these words, which yoke the theme of the previous chapter to that of this: 'there is a correspondence between topology and practice. This correspondence consists of time. Topology resists, and that's why the correspondence exists.'[2] Through interrogations into temporality and resistance, this chapter primarily focuses on what might be called one of the 'dialects' of psychosis—schizophrenia—in its relation to time, and societal power structures and relations, through a close reading of a clinical case study.

Psychoanalysis as a *praxis* is liable to receiving criticism (and has) due to what may be perceived as its insistence, reliance, and concentration on *the individual* (and by—something of a false—proxy, on *individualism* per se). Counterarguments of course concern psychoanalysis' situating of the individual in a social context, whether it be in the family, in some specific community setting, in society at large (or a combination of some or all of these, or more); and this is the case, to whatever extent, with all brands of the practice. What is susceptible to being overlooked should both of these instances become polarised, however, is the *taking of both of them* into account *by psychoanalysis*, in an *overdetermined* sense, in their truly *radical* dimensions; that is, *one is* truly an individual—an 'existent', as Emmanuel Levinas phrased it, completely separate from each other existent, whilst of course partaking of *existence—and one is* a social, and socially constructed, being: ineluctably, inescapably, and inextricably linked to, and linked by, the social structure.[3] It is Freud's—perhaps underappreciated—concept of *overdetermination* that allows of these two radical incompatibilities residing alongside one another, within (a) thereby riven subjectivity.[4]

DOI: 10.4324/9781003185239-4

Lacan argued that the human organism is in effect always 'born prematurely': one does not come into the world with any understanding of it, and of its specific systematicities; one is born *into* language, but *without it*; one does not have a preloaded database of all the mores and customs, morals and laws, etiquettes and expected behaviours, words, and signs and signals with which to make one's urges, needs, wants, desires, and drives known, but has to acquire the rudimentary *savoir faire* with which to negotiate these mindfields.[5] Thus it is that (individual) time, which radically begins with one's birth, is very much out of joint with that (continuing time) *into which* one is born (but is nonetheless inextricable from it). *Individual* time and *social* time in this respect can be put into the positions of sides 1 and 2 in the unificatory/separatory principle, with *temporality*—in the fullness of its Heideggerian meaning—filling position A.[6] This specific disjunctive temporal phenomenon will henceforward be referred to by the term 'enverneity'. One of the places in psychoanalysis in which enverneity arises is in the question concerning *duration*, and of what determines the (in)famous *longue durées* of (an) analysis: whilst 'the unconscious is located outside time'—as Lacan puts it, in a neat contraction of Freud's repeated insistence on its 'timelessness'—resistances are *precisely temporal*; that is, they are in effect a temporal 'muscular armouring', to adopt and adapt a phrase of Reich's, wrapped around an atemporal kernel, or navel; the unconscious itself.[7] The complicatedness or counterintuitiveness of what's involved here is demonstrated in the necessity of having to employ a spatial metaphor to describe a mechanism of time, as Freud famously did in his description of the eternal city in *Civilisation and Its Discontents*.[8]

Beyond psychoanalysis—within the psycho*social* itself—the *enverneous* can commonly be seen, for example, in the disjunctures of generationality and of ancestry. Take the instance of historical apology: a figurehead is called upon to make a public apology for the inhumanity and criminality of previous generations, of which by some link she is a representative; a member of an infamous family apologises for the deplorable actions of those of whom he is a descendent. This gesture is perceived as immediately necessary or vital, but there may also seem to be something lacking or futile in it. In terms of social justice, it is necessitous, in terms of recognition, of some power's—a nation's, government's, religious institution's, organisation's—wrongdoing, and as an attempt at reparation. Yet, in this instance, it remains the case that the individuals who committed the atrocities have not apologised themselves, that they in effect remain *unapologetic*. Between authenticity and inauthenticity, between full and empty speech and gesture, the figurehead or ancestor, and the historical predicament, is caught; the truth, in effect, can only be *half-said*, as Lacan put it.

What are at play and at stake here are the breaks-flows of historicity. The veracity of Deleuze and Guattari's term here finds its fullness in that if we ally the (emergence of each) individual with breaks (the historical ruptures of *beginning-(and ultimately ending-)times*) and the social with flows (the planes of *continuing-times*), the very *interconstitutivity* of the hyphen (or borderline) which unites–separates them is demonstrable. The at-onceness of breaks-flows renders enverneity intelligible again in this instance, but it will now be to where a further incongruity in the structure takes place that we will turn—which goes only to show up the function of enverneity all the more explicitly—through what we hope it will not be too daring to call a schizoanalysis, of the second family R. D. Laing and Aaron Esterson presented in their co-authored work *Sanity, Madness and the Family* (1964), the Blairs. The condensation of the long work with the patient into Laing and Esterson's brief survey, and my further contraction of it in the précises here given, will of course set us up at several removes in some respects; however—and firmly in the spirit of the original study—attentiveness to the language and discourses in use and at play within the family, the hospital, and the conditions of the observations and interviews, should prove illustrative of processes such as we are endeavouring to uncover. As the authors put it: 'our intention remains focused on rendering the 'schizophrenia' of this one person intelligible in the light of the family system, its praxis and process'.[9]

Hokum and bunkum: foreclosure

There is an irony in the pseudonym chosen for the young woman who is the central subject of this case study; she is named 'Lucie', yet—after twelve years of hospitalisation (ten full years, and two 'in and out')—she is almost as in the dark and still in search of enlightenment and lucidity as she has been throughout her thirty-eight years of life. She appears somewhat stuck in this subject position, as something of a *living* archaism. For Lucie, the time seems perpetually out of joint; she is unable to situate herself in it, riven with such an existential doubt, preventing her from ontologising temporally; even threatening to *de-ontologise* her temporally, to *desubjectivise* her.

In the temporal loci of her speech, she flits between tenses, being seemingly only able to figure the future with recourse to a qualifying *anterior* ('if I were to do A, B might happen'), which negates the possibility of the fantasised alterative action taking place, its counteraction being figured, and thus enacted, in advance.[10] She is rent, too, from the present and propelled back to the past by her mother's speech—as Mrs Blair constructs a hypothesised modern child (who is figured in the present tense) as a measure of comparison for Lucie (who is given past-tense signifiers, illustrated below by my italicisations)—even to the point of ending the sentences her mother begins in this respect, and thereafter claiming responsibility for the content of her mother's imputations (which she is subsequently confirmed in by her mother):

MOTHER: [...] I mean a child would see that it *was* a lot of bunkum.
INTERVIEWER: You say a child would see it was a lot of bunkum?
MOTHER: Well—the present day child *does*.
INTERVIEWER: I wonder why Miss Blair didn't see it.
MOTHER: Well I suppose she was brought up to put herself in the back—
LUCIE: Yes I think I put myself in the background. I stifled myself as it were, really stifled myself—snuffed my candle out—a horrible thing really, because if I said anything I was afraid of getting a clout, or something, you know what I mean?
MOTHER: Oh yes. [my italics][11]

Throughout the case study much recurs in terms of temporal and epochal comparison, both in historical time and within the family history, as it is constructed and narrativised, itself. (Both of these come at once in Mrs Blair's description of Mr Blair having 'to watch over [Lucie] all the time, like going back into Victorian days'.[12]) These instances will be teased out in this analysis, which will specifically focus on patriarchy and the lot of women, the disjunctural centrality and centrifugal dysfunction of which in this family's account implies something of a foreclosure, and failure of representation, that has resulted in mystification, and the disjointedness of enverneity.

In a later discussion concerning the Head family, Laing and Esterson state: 'the child [...] is born into [...] rights–obligations, duties, loyalties, rewards–punishments, already in existence, and much of his or her childhood training is necessarily taken up with parental techniques of inducing interiorization of this whole system'.[13] In the case of the Blairs, the overbearing father is depicted at every turn as the bearer of the Law, but the tablets on which it is inscribed, which are to be interiorised, remain enigmatic:

Father is the kind of character that wants you to do things and at the same time he's nervous of you doing them. He's so contradictory. He's got a contradictory attitude in his regard for women.

Figure 3.1 Positional demonstration: production of foreclosure.

He doesn't like men supporting women, and at the same time he doesn't like women to support themselves.[14]

This contradictoriness runs through the statements and injunctions of the father throughout the case study. A certain foreclosure seems to come out of contradictory statement (or action) A residing alongside—and being given equal weighting to—contradictory statement (or action) B. Indeed, the workings of this process can be schematised (as in Figure 3.1) along such lines.

This foreclosure thus seems to come about through the elision of *structural* patriarchy, a term we must take in its most current sense, in use in reference to the operations of structural racism and sexism, highlighted in the vicissitudes of social relations and machinations, and in governmental policy and procedure, for example. Like the unconscious itself, *the structural*—structuration as such—covers its tracks; involved in it is the 'overlooking of its own form', as Slavoj Žižek has put it, in relation to the unconscious.[15] For this reason we have put foreclosure in the below position above (we can add this to our schematic taxonomy as 'position B'), as stemming from the combinatory of contradictory statements (or actions), in that position A—weren't it hidden, or repressed—would be occupied by patriarchy itself, with its (antagonistic) self-contradictoriness resulting in statements A and B in positions 1 and 2. The distinction between repression and foreclosure here is of utmost importance, in that it is through *the father's* repression of the phenomenon (as such, *as declaredly what it is*) that structural patriarchy is foreclosed *to the daughter*. The repressed content of the father entails its foreclosure for the daughter (despite whatever allusions the mother might make to the phenomenon, as will be discussed momentarily). Figure 3.1 might thus be re-presented as Figure 3.2.

To elucidate these complicated workings of enverneity, we will launch into a survey of instances in which they come to the fore in the text. Of Mr Blair, Mrs Blair states: 'he wasn't prepared to be a husband. Just wanted me to be the nurse to the children. Something beneath him'.[16] Then, in a slightly later account, she claims of him:

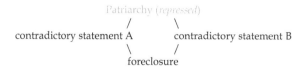

Figure 3.2 Positional demonstration: production of foreclosure from repression.

he's gone quite neurotic. You mustn't talk until he wants to be spoken to. He was harsh to Lucie. For no earthly reason he'd fly into a temper. He once gave her a terrific bang and next morning there was a terrific red patch on her back.[17]

She ends this testimony with a description of Mr Blair's family as 'far and away behind the times with their attitude towards women.'[18] Extracting the behaviour of Mr Blair from these statements, it would appear that he would act in a certain way domestically without providing justifications for his doing so, a behavioural baselessness likely presenting enigmatic signification for Lucie: looking after children was seemingly 'below him', he wasn't to be talked to unless it was requested by him, he would fly into rages, but 'for no earthly reason'. Patriarchal power is wielded by the father but is never identified by him *as such*. Without this explicitness from Mr Blair, Mrs Blair's words to the effect of denouncing his—and his family's—attitude towards women might be intelligible to Lucie, yet properly unassimilable, sans a fatherly signifier for them through which they could hook onto the unconscious. Beyond this, Lucie and her mother agree that when her father 'is present her mother must side with him', leaving even less room for Lucie to fully integrate her mother's denunciations.[19] This oedipal scene is thus the way in which the enverneity—of experiencing patriarchal dominance and injustices (in individual time), whilst not being plugged into the knowledge of structural patriarchy (in, and of, continuing social time)—plays itself out in the Blair 'family romance', as presented in the text. Indeed, as Laing and Esterson succinctly put it: from this, Lucie 'has no adequate vocabulary', and is often left 'mistrusting the fabric of her experience.'[20]

Due also to this operation of enverneity, when Lucie is home, Mrs Blair 'cannot bear to see the close bond between Lucie and her husband'.[21] Despite all her protestations against him—due likely to the above-identified unassimilable, *unsuturable*, foreclosure—Lucie remains much attached to her father, and he to her: a unificatory–separatory bond that may be perceived mystificatorily by its very participants, and may remain mystifying to its observers, unanalysed. Of all that may be bound up in this unconsciously, Laing and Esterson remind us in a note: 'we are fully alive to the inferences to which these facts point, namely Mr Blair's struggle with his unconscious incestuous feelings towards Lucie, her mother's jealousy of Lucie and her husband, and Lucie's own sexual attachment to her father'.[22] But beyond this oedipalisation—however acute—the time is yet out of joint: individual, familial attachment to the father is underwritten by social duty to the patriarch. The knowledge of the latter of these is thus foreclosed and perceived only to be partaking of something involved in the former.

This order of things is so deeply ingrained that its patriarchal dominance is inscribed into the very fabric and workings of Mr Blair's extended family—whom Mrs Blair describes as 'sort of sit[ting] in judgement' over the nuclear family—with its female actors becoming adjuncts in the functioning of its patriarchal order, or more precisely, *ordering* (of relations to suit that patriarchal order).[23] Whilst the descriptions of Lucie's aunt might read as in fact highlighting a higher form of matriarchy predominating in the household, whilst she had a stake in it (prior to her death), it can be argued—through paying heed to the fact that this very predominance sits squarely on the familial side of the father—that this rather speaks to the logic found, for example, in Lacan's formulae of sexuation, in which on the sides of the masculine and feminine (as structural positions) can be found either male or female subjects (i.e., here, on the side of the patriarchal is found the domineering aunt).[24] Indeed, the powerful injunction to respect this aunt comes directly from the father, in a manoeuvre of further denigration of Lucie's birth-mother: 'the children were told by Mr Blair to look to their aunt, while Mrs Blair was treated as their nurse', echoing the above statement concerning how Mrs Blair perceived her husband positioning her in relation to their children.[25] The patriarchal father in effect *metonymises* into his blood relations, himself a synecdoche of the patriarchal side of the family. This evocation of a privileged *side*, which seeks hegemony, brings us back to the tussling (a form of position A's inherent *antagonism*) involved in the principle of enverity: for example, position 1, of Mr Blair's side of the family, is attempting to claim proprietorship of position A (sought as a hegemonising function), over and against position 2: that of Mrs Blair and Lucie. That this is in operation is mystificatorily presented by Mr Blair (unconsciously, no doubt) as a lot of 'hokum' and 'bunkum'—to annex Mrs Blair's words—in an act of foreclosure that follows preset lines of *enverneity*.

Big bad wolves: disavowal

Lucie suffers from an 'inability to find significant others with authority to confirm or validate her point of view';

> she says she mistrusts her experience because she is weak-willed, and that she cannot evaluate the words and actions of others, or even be sure that they are saying anything at all. Yet she tends to believe what other people tell her even if she thinks they are wrong. This she calls weakness of will. She feels sometimes that it might be due to lack of confirmation, but she is not sure whether her experiences are not confirmed because they are in fact incorrect as her mother and father continually tell her.[26]

Above, we have identified a certain foreclosure operating in the relations between Mr Blair and Lucie (arising out of repressions in and enacted by Mr Blair); on the other side of this—on the father's part (and transmissionally)—is the process of disavowal (which we will discover taking the form of displacement). The fallout of this for Lucie is her confusion—what Laing and Esterson refer to throughout as her mystification—which she is loath to impute to others (through fear of punishment: 'clouts' and 'hidings')—and which we see her internalising, for example, in her self-reproaches against her 'weakness of will' (a symptom she seems to perceive as something bodily, in the sense elucidated in the previous chapter, in relation to the psychotic structure). To the psychiatric gaze this is Lucie's manifestations of 'thought-disorder', which Laing and Esterson disambiguate in a remarkable passage highlighting what we could term the institutional *schizophrenisation* of Lucie's situation, and person:

> This thought-disorder is the attempt by Lucie to describe events which are ambiguous and which she is sometimes not able to conceptualize clearly[.] She could hardly be expected to conceptualize them since they are not currently conceptualized adequately, either in any scientific language or in the colloquialisms of naïve psychology[.] The structure of the events she is trying to describe is intrinsically difficult for anyone to perceive and describe adequately, by virtue of their ambiguity, and, further, she is trying to perceive and remember just those things that she feels (in our view probably correctly) that she has been persistently punished for perceiving.[27]

Punishment encircles Lucie, and was received occasionally in a direct form meted out by her father, but more often, and more insidiously, it

lingered in a disavowed form displaced onto 'others', the 'outside': the ever-present and lurking ominousness and threat of 'big bad wolves': *men*. To make these parallel punishments clear, we will here parse a list of expectations and beliefs ('rewards–punishments', as Laing and Esterson would later call them) that her father laid out in his interview with the clinicians, and will group them into two 'phases':
Phase 1:

- There had always been a place for her at home.
- Mr Blair would not have her in the house for one year after she had been pregnant and forbade any mention of the episode, or any mention of her child. He also forbade his wife to see the child.
- His daughter was made to be a gentlewoman[;] a pure, virginal, spinster gentlewoman.
- His occasional physical and frequent verbal violence towards her were prompted by his view of her as sexually wanton. [...] By her sexuality his daughter betrayed him.

Phase 2:

- She could go down to the local shops any time she wished.
- Going out at night was, of course, another matter[, entailing] dangers [...] of being kidnapped or raped.
- He felt it unsafe for any woman to go any distance alone, especially at night.
- Her father believed that the district, a middle-class suburb, was infested by gangs of marauding youths, day and night[.] The *others* outside the family, the 'Them' who were the concern of Mr Blair, were all alike for him. None could be trusted. They were all men. [Lucie] could not be trusted, she was 'no better than they were', and so on.[28]

Phase 1 represents those contradictions creative of the foreclosure discussed in the first section of this chapter. The effects of this reach their peak in the period of expulsion from the house after Lucie's pregnancy and child-bearing, in which 'she did not find any greater freedom. The original situation appeared to have been sufficiently internalized for her to be unable to use the relative absence of constraints in the external world, outside her family'.[29] The infected view of what is outside the family, and what the external world is, is of course contaminated by the statements in the second phase. Indeed, phase 2 describes the disavowals of Mr Blair's own patriarchal omnipresence and omnipotence. The different operations in these phases might hint at qualitative differences in the father's uneasiness with elements of his masculine performativity; in phase 1 he may repress the explicitness of structural patriarchy, but is nonetheless happy to wield (its) power; yet in phase 2, he disavows any semblance of masculine sexuality, displacing it disdainfully onto others (not only the men 'out there', but even onto his own daughter).

Through her father's 'overprotectiveness', as Laing and Esterson put it: 'Lucie was cut off from both men and women, since she could not discriminate ordinary friendliness from imminent rape'.[30] Her father's disavowal into the outside world—and especially into other men—of aspects of sexuality that he *avowedly* found deplorable would go on to create the status or self-image in Lucie of the old oxymoronic and non-sensical playground taunt of 'frigid slut' (a signifier, incidentally, used today for women by a significant group of men finding identificatory relatedness in the ideology bemoaning the lot, and championing the resentment, of the 'beta male').

In contrast to the contradictions in the name of the father that create the severity of the foreclosure of (full recognition of the effects of) structural patriarchy, the effects of his disavowals onto the myth-ical ravenous men around every corner create the contradictions *within herself* that Lucie directly experiences. She is most aware of this, and yet again seems consistently unable to *assume* it, whilst identifying pre-cisely why this is so (it has been made *unconscious*; thus it would perhaps be touchable by analytic work—could that become available—beyond the family and the hospital: the *venerable institutions of schizophrenia/ schizophrenisation*). To leave the last transcribed words to Lucie herself:

> He's put that into my mind, my subconscious mind – that I can't be trusted, and I'll always be – you know – the big bad wolf will come after me – the world is full of big bad wolves – he's got that impregnated into my brain in some way, into my subconscious mind. And occasionally it seems to come to the surface all the time, you know – that the world is full of big bad wolves.[31]

Lucie knows full well that another world is possible, but, all the same, hers is upside-down; that the time is now, but, all the same, it is out of joint. If she has an inkling that that other world is out there, that it exists in the macrocosmic spatial conjuncture she belongs to, this is blocked by the version of the world that she is prescribed by the family (Laing and Esterson: 'what in clinical terms would be regarded as a typically paranoid world, is Mrs Blair's as much as her husband's'), and that is reinforced by her psychiatric internment. If she can envisage the time of emancipation, it is impeded by the operation of enverneity that unites her to it whilst separating her from it: '*occasionally* it comes to the surface *all the time*.' This operation of enverneity seems to leave her stuck with that eternal internal and infernal determining question: 'what's the time, Mr Wolf?'

Notes

1 A version of this chapter has appeared as Daniel Bristow, 'Enverneity: A Close Reading of the Blair Family Case Study in Laing and Esterson's *Sanity, Madness and the Family', European Journal of Psychotherapy & Counselling*, 23rd ser., 1 (2021) 70–84.

2 Jacques Lacan, *The Seminar of Jacques Lacan, Book XXVI: Topology and Time, 1978–1979*, trans. by Dan Collins (Unofficial translation, n.d.) p.1.

3 Much in Levinas' phrasing resonates with our notions of unificatory/ separatoriness. For example, in 'the adherence of existence to an existent appear[ing] like a cleaving', and of 'an existent's adherence to existence, in which their separation already begins'. See Emmanuel Levinas, *Existence and Existents* [1947], trans. by Alphonso Lingis (Pittsburgh: Duquesne University Press, 2001) p.9 and p.10.

4 'As a rule the neuroses are *overdetermined*; that is to say, several factors operate together in their aetiology.' See Sigmund Freud, 'A Reply to Criticisms of My Paper on Anxiety Neurosis' [1895], trans. by J. Rickman, in *SE*, III, p.131. On the use of the word 'incompatible' in this same volume, see James Strachey's footnote in 'The Neuro-Psychoses of Defence' [1894], trans. by J. Rickman, in ibid. p.51, n.4.

5 See Jacques Lacan, 'The Mirror Stage as Formative of the *I* Function as Revealed in Psychoanalytic Experience' [1949], in *Écrits*, p.78.

6 'Temporality "is" not an *entity* at all. It is not, but it *temporalizes* itself. [...] Temporality temporalizes, and indeed it temporalizes possible ways of itself. [...] *Temporality is the primordial 'outside-of-itself' in and for itself.* We therefore call the phenomena of the future, the character of having been, and the Present, the '*ecstases*' of temporality.' See Martin Heidegger, *Being and Time* [1927], trans. by John Macquarrie and Edward Robinson (Malden, MA: Blackwell, 1962) p.377. These attributes of temporality of course resonate with Lacan's later concepts of *ex-sistence* and *extimacy*.

7 See Jacques Lacan, *The Seminar of Jacques Lacan, Book I: Freud's Papers on Technique, 1953–1954*, ed. by Jacques-Alain Miller, trans. by John Forrester (New York: W. W. Norton, 1988) p.243; Sigmund Freud, 'The Unconscious' [1915], trans. by C. M. Baines et al., in Freud, *SE*, XIV, p.187; Reich, *Character Analysis*, pp.337–352.

8 See Freud, *Civilization and Its Discontents* [1930], trans. by Joan Riviere, in Freud, *SE*, XXI, pp.70–71.

9 R. D. Laing and Aaron Esterson, *Sanity, Madness and the Family*, p.26.

10 'LUCIE: Well I think my mother was one to be reproached, but I worry about it. I feel that she'd be too hurt about it, or she'd give me – give me a good hiding.' See ibid. p.48.

11 Ibid.

12 Ibid., p.49.

13 Ibid., p.167.

14 Ibid., p.47.

15 See Slavoj Žižek, *Less Than Nothing* (London: Verso, 2012) p.485.

16 Laing and Esterson, *Sanity, Madness and the Family*, pp.27–28.

17 Ibid., pp.29–30.

18 Ibid., p.30.

19 Ibid., p.31.

20 Ibid., p.34, and p.41.

21 Ibid., p.50.

22 Ibid., p.30, note.

23 Ibid., p.32.

24 See Lacan, *Seminar XX: Encore.*

25 Laing and Esterson, op. cit.

26 Ibid., p.40.

27 Ibid., p.34. In Maud Mannoni's perspicacious reading of Laing and Esterson's book she summates: 'the family [...] reflects the position of classical psychiatry: there is no room in it for a subject.' See Maud Mannoni, *The Child, his 'Illness', and the Others* [1967], [trans. by unknown] (Harmondsworth: Penguin University Books, 1973) p.102, n.7.

28 All quotations taken from Laing and Esterson, *Sanity, Madness and the Family*, p.43.

29 Ibid.

30 Ibid., p.44.

31 Ibid., p.38.

4 Class (Antagonism)

(Divisions in materiality and distribution: between the Lacanian orders)

In 1935, Hsi Tseng Tsiang self-published his novel *The Hanging on Union Square*, the first act of which ends in this set of stanzas:

> He is a radical; he has no money.
> He is conservative; he has money.
> He is wishy-washy; he has a wishy-washy amount of money.
>
> He has more money; he is more conservative.
> He has more more money; he is more more conservative.
> He has more more and more money; he is more more and more conservative.
> He has no money. Yet he is conservative. He expects someday to have money. He expects someday to have lots of money.
> He has money. He has lots of money. Yet he is radical. Radical talk costs him no money.
> I don't like money. You don't like money. He doesn't like money.
>
> It's under this system!
> It's under this system!
>
> Mr. System
> Beware.[1]

Setting the scene for these concluding remarks, the attempt is made in this last chapter to bring the preceding work of this book into relation with the fields of political economy, dialectical materialism, and class antagonism, via a psychoanalytic engagement.

DOI: 10.4324/9781003185239-5

Primary and secondary processes

In the preface to *A Contribution to a Critique of Political Economy* (1859), Marx makes one of his most significant interventions, in the brief discussion of how 'the totality of th[e] relations of production constitute [...] the economic structure of society, the real foundation, on which arises a legal and political superstructure, and to which correspond[s] definite *forms of social consciousness*'.[2] From this has arisen the distinction—so dear to classical, and 'vulgar', Marxism— of 'base and superstructure', apparatuses somewhat similar to Freud's 'primary' and 'secondary processes', which the latter deems 'theoretical fictions', in *The Interpretation of Dreams* (1899).[3] Marx returns to and defends this line of thinking in volume one of *Capital* (and develops it at further length in the section on labour rent in volume three)—in a fascinating and excoriating footnote—citing as an example of the dialectic between the specificity of the economic conditions and pro- ductive relations of any given time and its judicial, political, and cul- tural superstructure, 'Don Quixote, who long ago paid the penalty for wrongly imagining that knight errantry was compatible with all eco- nomic forms of society'.[4] Thus, for Marx, modern 'consciousness must be explained from the contradictions of [its] material life, from the con- flict existing between the social forces of production and the relations of production'.[5] The material contradictions—and their playing-out in the split consciousness, divided subjectivity and subjection, and exist- ential conflicts and struggles of class—are thus the forms that the antagonistic structure in the (economic) base of things takes. In his esti- mate of attempts made by rival camps to elide antagonism itself, Marx concludes: 'we might just as well try to retain Catholicism without the Pope'.[6]

Indeed, we can see the structuration of both enverity and enverneity come into focus here: firstly, in the antagonistic structure (A), *the totality of relations of production*, that gives rise to its substratum (1), *economic conditions*, and superstratum (2), *social relations*; and secondly, in the temporal disjuncture between what we could reterm 'base' time, *indi- vidual* temporality, determined as it is by personal economic circum- stance, and 'superstructural' time, *social* temporality, determined as the conjuncture that encrusts itself culturally, judicially, and politically (with Don Quixote's out-of-jointness positioning him similarly—albeit more comically (a mode allowed to him by his particular time)—to Lucie in Laing and Esterson's study). Reading Marx closely here teaches us to avoid the 'vulgar Marxist' mistake that Reich draws attention to in *The Mass Psychology of Fascism* (1933), of deriving from this model 'a mechanical antithesis between economy and ideology, between 'structure' and 'superstructure' [, one that] makes ideology rigidly and one-sidedly dependent on economy, and fails to see the dependency of economic development upon that of ideology'.[7] Indeed, Marxian materialism would not be properly *dialectical* without recognition of such codependencies.

Such vulgarity tends to lead to confusions of economic, political, and sociocultural relations; of affectual (and genetic), familial, and structural (clinical, or 'nosographical') relations; and to the mistaking of classes themselves for attributes popularly and caricaturally ascribed to them. These confusions are often purposefully made and propounded by those in power—to reinforce and rule over the class divisions that they promulgate—and are taken up, and handed down, from one generation to another, through processes of misrecognition, or in accordance with lumpen, and unconscious (un-*class-conscious*) psychical structures. In the foundational essay 'Dialectal Materialism and Psychoanalysis' (1929), Reich sifts certain of these economico-ideological phenomena and divisions in structure, and filters them through a precise psychosocial reading:

> Reduced to the most simple formula, the economic structure of society—through many intermediary links such as the class association of the parents, the economic conditions of the family, its ideology, the parents' relationship to one another, etc.—enters into a reciprocal relation with the instincts, or ego, of the newborn. Just as his ego changes his environment, so the changed environment reacts upon his ego. There arises a contradiction between the instinctual needs and the social order, of which the family (and later the school) act as the representative. This contradiction produces a conflict which leads to a change, and as the individual is the weaker opponent, the change occurs within his psychological structure.[8]

We might here return to the instance with which we began this work: the disagreement between Reich and Freud regarding the death drive. It relates precisely to considerations of class and its attributes in that in his early period Reich was consistent in analysing the vicissitudes of psychosocial mass structure (neuroses derived from the authoritarian family setup) as a secondary process occurring as change to and within the individual psychological structure. This is what he carried over from his perspicacious study and penetrating understanding of the early Freud; namely, the conceptualisation of primary and secondary processes, for the first of which Freud states:

What I had in mind was not merely considerations of relative importance and efficiency; I intended also to choose a name which would give an indication of its chronological priority. It is true that, so far as we know, no psychical apparatus exists which possesses a primary process only, and that such an apparatus is to that extent a theoretical fiction. But this much is a fact: the primary processes are present in the mental apparatus from the first, while it is only during the course of life that the secondary processes unfold.[9]

This unfolding of the secondary processes Reich reads back to and against Freud, and his concept of death drive. In his controversial essay on masochism, included in *Character Analysis*, Reich summarises Freud's original conception of the origin of masochism:

> Sadism becomes masochism when it is turned against the person himself; the superego (the representative of the person responsible for frustration or, to put it another way, the representative of the demands of society in the ego) becomes the agent of punishment toward the ego (conscience). The guilt feeling results from the conflict between the love striving and the destructive impulse.
> The concept that masochism is a secondary formation was later given up by Freud.[10]

Reich retains the concept where Freud summons the death drive. The divergence on this point led not only to Reich's eventual expulsion from the International Psychoanalytical Association and the finality of his break with Freud, but even to an attempt on Freud's part to denounce Reich's rejection of the death drive as being in the service of his commitment to Communism, amounting to an intriguing (re)positioning of Eros, and the life-force (for the Left).[11] In effect, arraying his thought against the terms of Freud's schema of primary and secondary process provided Reich with a cartography for assessing structuration. Such could thus be adopted to put paid to those notions of class—and class prejudices—which mistake effects for causes; differences for stereotypes; personal circumstances for political positions; cultural for financial capital; idiosyncrasies (of dress, comportment, character, etc.) for class inherencies, and so on. In each instance, the primary process involved in the relations of the productive forces that constitute economic conditions goes on to produce the secondary process involved in class distinction and differentiation.

It is important to separate primary from secondary here in that it can mitigate against particular misguided notions, such as those that

are wont to read in Pierre Bourdieu's concept of 'cultural capital'—
outlined in his magisterial 1979 work, *Distinction*—an equal material
weighting to *economic capital*, for example. Bourdieu is precise in a
delineation he gives in the book of how an 'internalized code called culture functions as cultural capital owing to the fact that, being unequally
distributed, it secures profits of distinction'.[12] Presenting as 'cultured'
relies on the internalisation of a set of coded practices and relations,
which can allow one to seamlessly manoeuvre within the classed hab-
itus (and classed socius), and thus functions as a form of 'capital'. This
bears itself out in the psychoanalytic clinic in ways in which Joanna
Ryan describes in her 2017 work, *Class and Psychoanalysis*:

> The denial or sidelining of economic factors in favour of cultural
> distinctions is something that the psychoanalytic field is likely to be
> prone to, especially given the legacy of exclusion of working-class
> people from psychoanalysis on grounds of their supposed lack of
> verbal ability and educational credentials—that is, their cultural
> capital.[13]

It is this very *internalisation* of which Bourdieu speaks, however,
that is the secondary process; secondary to 'the economic structure of
society' (and the *economic* position in which one finds oneself within
this) from which it takes its bearing: the primary process, or 'the real
foundation', as Marx has it.[14] This isn't merely confirmed in singular or
anomalous figures that we might conjure up, from the 'cultured pauper'
to the 'queer class subject'—as 'exceptions that prove the rule'—but
more materially, and consequentially, in the fact that if we reverse the
processes it can lead to the phenomenon we see so often in late capitalism in which the notion of cultural capital has become well enough
understood, subsumed, or unconsciously absorbed, to be cynically
mobilised in attempts to *substitute* for monetary, remunerative (wage)
capital, as is endlessly exampled in the proletariat's degradation to the
status of precariat, which works (slaves) often only for the reward of
cultural capital, receiving, as it has begun to, only virtual 'payment';
that of *experience*, or *opportunity*—of bolstering CVs, networking, 'job
satisfaction' as trade-off for a real living wage—in the era of zero-hours
contracts, unpaid internships, and gig economy.[15] Edward Bernays eat
your heart out.

Whilst this separation-out into primary and secondary process proves
useful and utilisable (to such instances), it yet runs the risk of collapsing
back into the non-dialectical vulgar Marxism of which we need to be

ever-wary, unless it is further qualified. In this respect, a rejuvenation of Lacan's three orders may serve here as something of a salve. Before we venture onto this territory, we will leave the last dialectical materialist word on primari- and secondariness with Reich himself:

> If I want to call a strike for example, I cannot go direct to the machines but must understand the worker, win him over, inform him, gain his conviction, overcome his inhibitions against striking and so on. Once I have grasped the psychological structure of man, which is shaped by the economic structure—and only in this sense can we admit the primacy of economic factors—then I can also grasp the economy, and by mastering the economy, in turn, I change again the human psychological structure. Anyone who cannot see this has no business to call himself a Marxist. The economist has it thus: the economy gives rise to consciousness. Economic propaganda, therefore, means talking about shops, and crises of production, whereas psychological propaganda means talking about emotions and private life. This conception brought about our defeat and now threatens the Soviet Union. The dialectical materialist does not see the economy on the one hand and man on the other, but sees man through the economy and at the same time the economy through man. The economic structure is for him the external condition ultimately determining life, constituted in reality in the form of natural and synthetic productive forces, in the labour power of men and in their needs. The acts, feelings and desires of men are the first condition—not the prime determinate of being. The economic structure is external to man, but brought into being and directed by him: once created, it is subject to its own laws, which work precisely like the laws of nature. Just as a psychology without an economy is an idea without content, an economy without psychological preconditions, without an active human mind, is the conception of an impossibility—something dead, which is supposed to live without containing life.[16]

The Real, the Symbolic, and the Imaginary

'A certain analyst did once jokingly admit that while it was true that an airplane was a penis symbol, all the same it got you from Berlin to Vienna.' Reich recounts this amusing anecdote in 'Dialectical Materialism and Psychoanalysis'.[17] Expanding on it in the essay 'Psychoanalysis in the Soviet Union' (1929), he assesses this propensity for oversymbolisation that runs rife in vulgar, symbolistic (nonclinical) psychoanalysis, against the *materialist* theory of Marxism:

> Marxist thinking, being absolutely materialist-orientated, resists not symbolism as such but its misuse; but then, so does the thinking of a clinical psychoanalyst. Every object and every activity has its rational meaning; it may become a symbol, but does not by any means have to become one. Objects and activities owe their existence, not to their symbolic meaning, but to their value as utility articles or commodities—or, in the case of activities, to productive work. Airplanes and railways are not made because they are symbols of instinctual ideas, but because certain production conditions lead to their being invented and made. What goes on in the designer's unconscious as he designs them is of importance only if he comes to us as a patient. And even if the airplane he has invented has some phallic significance for him, that does not mean that the symbol was the motive for making the airplane. In the fifth century, when phallic ideas were no different from what they are today, the same man could certainly not have designed an airplane. We have to admit that this argument, often advanced by Marxists, is objectively faultless.[18]

An extreme of such symbolisation—or symbolic projection—is offered by Reich in his recalling the analytic 'suggestion, offered in all seriousness, that capitalism is a matter of the instincts'.[19] Indeed, I have heard it suggested that the class system may be suited to being symbolised through Freud's second topography, with the proletariat as id; the bourgeoisie as ego; and the ruling, upper classes as superego.[20] Not only is this *essentialising* of the highest order, it puts certain (caricatural) characteristics, so easily convertible into so many prejudices— the 'impulsivity' and 'uninhibitedness' of the id; the 'refinement' and 'smoothness' of the ego (upon ideas of which the practice of ego-psychology—the therapeutic matching of the analysand's 'undeveloped' ego up to the analyst's 'developed' one—relies); the hard and fast rule of the superego—directly in the service of those who would benefit from being able to wield them as such (imagine UK Prime Minister Boris Johnson invoking a 'scientific psychology' to back up his comments concerning the 'drunk[eness], criminal[ity], aimless[ness], feckless[ness] and hopeless[ness]' of 'blue-collar men', for example).[21]

The battle over the Symbolic it is abundantly clear is immensely important, and determining, *politically*. It is the order hegemony over which will serve to guarantee perpetuations of representation however contrary to the conditions out of which they actually arise. This order and the Imaginary are thus prey to being eminently capitalised upon (*territorialised*) by the ruling classes, in order to cement and entrench their rule. An instance from Marx will settle things for the Imaginary in this divisory respect. It is that in which he talks of the credit system—in the third volume of *Capital*—in which 'the actual capital that someone possesses, *or is taken to possess by public opinion*, now becomes simply the basis for a superstructure of credit'.[22] Late capitalism might be described, in one conceptualisation at least, as precisely this *superstructure of credit—in toto*—its basis subsisting on the ideological retroactions of *public opinion*; 'the dependency of economic development upon that of ideology'—or *mass psychology*—in Reich's insightful words. A domestic counterpart might be found in the first volume of Tove Ditlevsen's *Copenhagen Trilogy* (1967–1971)—*Childhood*—in which there is a delightful passage that highlights the deep ideological impressions of authoritarian–familial structures, and all that gets wrapped up in them:

> Even though I know Sundholm is a place where you sleep on straw and get salt herring three times a day, the name goes into the verse I make up when I'm scared or alone, because it's beautiful like the picture in one of my father's books that I'm so fond of. It's called 'Worker family on a picnic', and it shows a father and mother and their two children. They're sitting on some green grass and all of them are laughing while they eat from the picnic basket lying between them. All four of them are looking up at a flag stuck into the grass near the father's head. The flag is solid red. I always look at the picture upside down since I only get a chance to see it when my father is reading the book. Then my mother turns on the light and draws the yellow curtains even though it's not dark yet. 'My father was a scoundrel and a drunkard,' she says, 'but at least he wasn't a socialist.'[23]

Imagine the granting of the autonomy to choose one's own *imaginary*. Through the Real—elided and kept hidden, due to its irruptive, disruptive, *revolutionary* potential—these orders might be deterritorialised, leaving them radically open, precisely to being *reterritorialised* through class struggle. Before cautiously hypothesising how, however, we must take heed of the warning Ryan draws attention to in her study:

> Class identifications and identities, as built on processes of distinction and repudiation, and on circulating social imaginaries

of various kinds, are only one aspect of how class operates, albeit a salient and prolific one. Rather we also need accounts of the formation of classed psyches in terms of the material circumstances and histories of different classes, and especially those of poverty, wealth and power; how class is embodied and transmitted in the earliest and continuing conditions of a child's social circumstances, and the kinds of class formations that follow from this. These material aspects have been much less explored psychoanalytically.[24]

In other words, *we mustn't forget our Marx*; and we should here hone our understanding of class psychoanalytically through the three Lacanian orders. A clarion call for clarity. Firstly, and fundamentally, we should recognise that capital—and distribution of wealth—occupies a similar position in (Marxian) economics as sex—and sexuality—does in (Freudian) psychoanalysis; that of the constitutive factor: which constructs the class system, and its formations; which constructs the nosological system, and its formations. These are systems and formations upon which superstructures and complexes are built, and systems and formations from which something is reflected back that seems to too sharply touch a nerve, triggering gargantuan mobilisations of reaction, resistance, repression, and foreclusion; of the kind that Tausk identifies in a typical counterrecommendation of:

> "Psychotherapy by reasonable analysis." It would not be surprising if "reasonable" in this context turns out to mean "non-sexual" or "almost non-sexual," as authors always fall back on "reason" when they wish to spare themselves the acknowledgement of any debt to Freud or psychoanalysis. It is regrettable that all that "reasonable" analysts know about the unconscious and everything connected with it comes from "unreasonable" psychoanalysis—an embarrassing situation for "reasonable" analysts, I must confess.[25]

Likewise with Marx's unveilings of the structuration of economic and productive forces. All such is gloriously consolidated in an image Alenka Zupančič gives, in riposte to Adam Smith's 'invisible hand of the market': that of the 'invisible handjob'; and indeed, as Reich hammered home, the revolution needs to be sexual as well as economic.[26]

In systematic and formational terms it would be as ill-judged as the above usage of the second topography to align classes themselves with the orders; no—instead, we should investigate where the constituents, components, and conditions that determine and codify class fall in relation to the orders, and where distribution of the types of capital that Ryan elucidates fall also; those of these

> approximate definitions: economic capital includes income, wealth, financial assets and inheritances. Cultural capital includes dispositions of mind and body, as in taste, style, etiquette, etc.; cultural goods; and educational and professional qualifications. Social capital includes resources built on networks of connection and affiliation, legitimated in the operations of power. All are context-specific.[27]

We will tabulate all such under the headings of the orders (as in Figure 4.1), and indicate, too, processual operations of primacy and secondariness within them, going on to delineate their inner and interrelational workings thereafter, thusly:

Real: We employ the Real here as a 'theoretical fiction'—as, properly, the real cannot be conceived of as a *reality*—but in line with Marx's designation of the 'real foundation', in terms of *economic* conditions, and, further, as that denoting the '*most real*' of the types of distribution, in that if one suffers the *primary* deprivations of unfavourable economic disparity, no amount of secondary 'capital' is going to supply for basic needs, of food, shelter, etc. Cultural capital don't pay the bills. (This, of course, might not be so if one suffers such deprivations *secondarily*, as is exampled in so many instances: of bankruptcies, which do nothing to impoverish the bankruptees; institutional bailouts, associated with the phenomenon of being 'too big to fail'; aristocrical property and asset-retention after loss or squandering of fortune, etc. Here it is

Real	*Symbolic*	*Imaginary*
Primary: Relations of production/economic conditions	*Primary*: Political/cultural representations	*Primary*: Affects/ideology
Secondary: Wealth/material distribution	*Secondary*: Cultural distribution	*Secondary*: Social/affectual distribution

Figure 4.1 RSI table with primary and secondary processes.

political secondariness—precisely, *political* economy; an all-pervasive and -evasive *credit system* apparatus in itself—that proves salvific.)

Symbolic: The Symbolic relies on narrative lines of *representation*; that is, on how the information it releases is politically *represented*. It operates according to its own semantic system, and it encodes its linguistics into the DNA of the institutions it assimilates, or appropriates: the media, for example, often repeat and reinscribe the ruling language. Culturally, if its language can be learned—beyond being inherited by heirs to its cultural capital—it can only be so by those to whom it is specifically taught, and it is only taught *by rote*.

Imaginary: The Imaginary often subsists in mystification and an assemblage of misrecognitions, such as that of one's regional accent for one's entire class subjectivity. The Nazi 'race ideology', which—in the preface to the third edition of *The Mass Psychology of Fascism*—Reich describes as '*a pure biopathic expression of the character structure*', and as '*biologic mysticism*', is refuted by him in the work 'only by exposing its irrational functions, of which there are essentially two: that of giving expression to certain *unconscious* and *emotional* currents prevalent in the nationalistically disposed man and of concealing certain psychic tendencies'.[28] As he says, it is useless to try to convince a fascist of the fallacy of a concept of racial inferiority or superiority; likewise, it can often be a difficult task to try to convince someone otherwise who has positioned one in class terms based solely on affectual phenomena or attributes; we can only expose these instances' irrationality.

Let us now synthesise the systematics of these, and then go on to describe their effects:

> *Real*: A system of economic disparities that privilege and are used to the advantage of the ruling classes.
> *Symbolic*: A system of codifications that structures the symbolic network of exchange and interchange.
> *Imaginary*: A system of unconscious and emotive structures that underwrite ideology and ideological assumptions.

The *effects* of each of the orders are directly *experienced*: the Symbolic, in policymaking that advantages the ruling class and advances its interests, disadvantaging the subjects over whom it rules; the Imaginary, in the prejudicial archetypes implanted into the unconscious and implemented in *intraclass* conflict; the Real, in poverty, malnutrition, illness and inaccessibility of healthcare, working and living

conditions, etc., and the maintenance of these, on which the maintenance of the capitalist system—and the energetics of crisis on which it
thrives—subsists. All of these effects can be *suffered*; and, so as to avoid
scaling suffering, we may maintain here the *oscillability* of the three
orders, in this respect.

Class is determined by the 'real' of economic conditions, and
relations of production. Its effects are experienced acutely and materially as a direct result of this; they are redoubled in mobilisations of the
imaginary, against particular groups—which get *classed* based on certain bodily and affectual markers—and which co-opts markers of race,
gender, sexuality, disability, etc., to further its (preset) programme; and it
is reinscribed by the symbolic setting-of-terms and framing-of-*situation*
(the manufacturing of forms of '*realism*'). Class struggle is structured
by the deep, inerasable antagonism at the heart of these fissures.

Working-through: permanent revolution

V. I. Lenin set out in *The State and Revolution* (1918) a map for *working-
through*: from capitalism, through socialism, to communism. There is
something similar in it to the process involved in psychoanalysis, from
which the term 'working-through' is borrowed in this paraphrase. It is a
lengthy and committed work, involving coming up against and pushing
through so many structural resistances; of laying the groundwork
of a 'royal road', which may lead to untold equilibria; it is a process
involving desire, *without concession*; traversal, of fundamental fantasies;
and yet it is one on which the jury's out as to whether it is terminable or
interminable. That it might—that it *can*—bring about *change* is vitally
important, however. If communistically it is the subject that is the force
with the potential to bring about collective change, psychoanalytically
the subject harbours the potential to bring about individual change: to
be *revolutionary*, the latter should play into the former; the individual
join the collective (struggle). As in transition to communism, so often it
is the case in psychoanalysis that the *last resistance*—if only before the
next—is that of *investment*, with all of the capitalistic overtones that
this entails.[29]

We will read this through a line that Laing is popularly cited as
having said: that 'there is a great deal of pain in life and perhaps the
only pain that can be avoided is the pain that comes from trying to avoid
pain', a paraphrase of the quotation from Franz Kafka that he uses as
an epigraph to the chapter entitled 'The inner self in the schizoid con-
dition' in *The Divided Self* (1960).[30] *We put ourselves in pain in trying
to avoid pain.* Some might see this as the formula of therapeutics: that

the re-experiencing of pain is necessitous to its dissolution. This is misguided, in that it misses the fundamental point here; that it is the pain of trying to avoid pain that is, *perhaps, avoidable*. *Perhaps*! (The 'perhaps' is in both Kafka and Laing.) *Imagine* the fiduciary strain of having only this *'perhaps'* to base the wager on; of having no *guarantee*. In Laing's statement there is a primary and a secondary pain. It is the accumulation of the primary pain that the subject becomes so invested *with*—and *has been* so invested with, over time, over the course of life—and of this secondary pain that they become so invested *in*. The primary pain is *guaranteed*; the secondary pain becomes accumulated over the course of its work (the work of therapy, the working-through of psychoanalysis). A therapeutic failure would be the invitation, the very *guaranteeing*, of a tertiary pain: precisely that pain *that might be avoided*. Indeed, the therapeutic *change* could be the offloading of (some of) that secondary pain, that secondary accumulation, secondary investment, although it might seem so hard to give up, in the absence of guarantees. Years of *working-through*—in the goal of alleviating the weight of all these years of work—might *come to naught*. *Imagine* giving up that investment in all this work. How we would resist that! Resist it with the foreboding premonition: 'what if… all that work, for nothing!'—but was that not the goal; the alleviation of that work, of the pain of that work?—instead, we might yet intone: 'not for nothing, all that work.' There is an *economic* psychical relation at play, and *psychical economy* is at stake, here.

Reich—of whom Laing was an admirer—writes in 'What Is Class Consciousness?' (1934):

> No bourgeois psychiatrist of average mentality will ever accept the view that neuroses, psychoses, addictions, etc., are consequences of the appalling sexual economy of the masses. The broad masses, on the other hand, are extremely interested in these problems, if only because they are a source of serious suffering for them and because the narrow-mindedness of the psychiatrists—those administrators of the capitalist sexual order—and the psychical misery resulting from it affect them personally and directly. I am sure that the average working-class youth has a better understanding of the relationship between repressed sexuality and psychical depression or loss of working capacity than most average psychiatrists throughout the world.[31]

The masses' access to their own problems—of political, psychical, and sexual economy—is barred, and the institutions of the bourgeoisie act (in the service of the ruling classes) as its gatekeepers. Recalibrating the economic conditions and productive relations that underwrite these (the distribution of wealth and class consciousness; the distribution of psychosocial aetiology; the distribution of sex education and awareness) might pave the way to revolution in each of these areas, and the reclaiming of divisions in structure, surface, and temporality.

After Marx and Engels, Leon Trotsky set out the theory of 'permanent revolution' (of which there can be no greater anti-conservatism) in which resides both the notion of achieving *permanency of the revolution*—how to make the revolution permanent, uninterruptedly and internationally; that is, beyond 'socialism in one country', and in relation to the state of world capitalism—and something of the preservation of the *perpetuity of revolutionariness*, integral to it; that is, the preservation of revolutionary *activation*, of its *working-through*.[32] To theorise this (diagrammatically, in Figure 4.2)—in terms of structure, topology, temporality, and class—we might return all the way to G. W. F. Hegel here, and reactivate the concept of *sublation*; that which *cancels and preserves, at once*.

Psychically (or, psy-economically), we might come to conceptualise the *sinthome* as the *sublated* symptom. If the *sinthome* is the *real* of the symptom, we might envisage the symptom's sublation as the dehiscence of its imaginary bearing (ideological investment), and the decathexis of its symbolic content, granting the subject the freedom to assign (new) meaning, and autonomy, to it (*sinthomically*; that is, in an act of 'self-writing', or 'auto-orthography'). Specific psychoanalytic (and sex-economic) schemas might be drawn up for each and every hysteric, obsessional, pervert, and psychotic—with all of their 'dialects', and 'regional accents'—of how to assume a place in (their own) *revolutionariness*; that of their individual analyses.

These unificatory/separatory sublations of *enverity* here map onto those of *enverneity*, in which temporal change is inaugurated—as Reich puts it—via the materialist

> dialectic[, which] resolves, without denying it, the contrast between evolution and revolution. A change in the social order is at first prepared by evolution (labor becoming a social process ['work-democracy'], the majority becoming proletarian, etc.) and then actually brought about by revolution.[33]

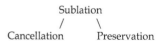

Figure 4.2 Positional demonstration: sublation.

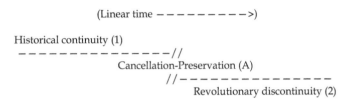

Figure 4.3 Positional demonstration: revolutionary temporality.

We may modify here how the great British thinker Stuart Hall sets out just these workings in his 1966 essay 'Political Commitment', in which he states that

> revolutions of different kinds transform and transpose—but they do not transform and transpose out of nothing: historical continuity is always preserved, and the means and methods of change which are adopted become in a sense the content of the transformation.[34]

In fact—*sublatively* (as depicted in Figure 4.3)—historical continuity is only preserved *in* revolutionary discontinuity; or, rather, it is *cancelled-preserved*, in that the continuing, diachronic superstructure of social time has had a radical and *singular* modification made in its synchronic base-time.

Within the ongoing revolutionary dialectic, we might trace such class-disestablishing coordinates as those of a state of Reichian 'work-democracy', transitioning through the Leninist dissolution of the 'state of democracy' itself—precisely, as *statist*—to the *sublation* of work itself (cancellation of defunct workings and preservation of functional *working-through*).[35] Political commitment, or fidelity, to all of which may take the form of a *permanent revolution*: the realisation—and assumption—of the divisions in structure, surface, temporality, and classification of subjectivity; of *enverity* itself.

Notes

1 H. T. Tsiang, *The Hanging on Union Square: An American Epic* [1935], ed. by Floyd Cheung (London: Penguin Classics, 2019) p.5.
2 Karl Marx, 'Preface (to *A Contribution to the Critique of Political Economy*)' [1859], in *Early Writings*, trans. by Rodney Livingstone and Gregor Benton (London: Penguin Classics, 1992) p.425.

3 Sigmund Freud, *The Interpretation of Dreams (Second Part)* [1899], trans. by James Strachey, in *SE*, V, p.603.

4 Karl Marx, *Capital: A Critique of Political Economy, Volume 1* [1867], trans. by Ben Fowkes, 3 vols (London: Penguin Classics, 1990) I, p.176, n.35. See Karl Marx, *Capital: A Critique of Political Economy, Volume III* [1894], trans. by David Fernbach, 3 vols (London: Penguin Classics, 1991) III, pp.925–930.

5 Marx, 'Preface (to *A Contribution to the Critique of Political Economy*)', in *Early Writings*, p.426.

6 Karl Marx, 'Marx's Selected Footnotes', in *Capital: An Abridged Edition*, p.484. For this in Fowkes' translation, see Marx, *Capital, Volume 1*, p.181, n.4.

7 Wilhelm Reich, *The Mass Psychology of Fascism* [1933/1942], trans. by Vincent R. Carfagno (Harmondsworth: Pelican Books, 1975) p.48.

8 Wilhelm Reich, 'Dialectical Materialism and Psychoanalysis' [1929/1934], in *Sex-Pol: Essays, 1929–1934* [1972], ed. by Lee Baxandall, trans. by Anna Bostock (London: Verso Radical Thinkers, 2012) pp.37–38.

9 Freud, *The Interpretation of Dreams (Second Part)*, p.603.

10 Reich, *Character Analysis*, pp.228–229.

11 See Reich, *Reich Speaks of Freud*, pp.134–137 and pp.217–222.

12 Pierre Bourdieu, *Distinction: A Social Critique of the Judgement of Taste* [1979], trans. by Richard Nice (Abingdon: Routledge Classics, 2010) p.555, n.4.

13 Joanna Ryan, *Class and Psychoanalysis: Landscapes of Inequality* (Abingdon: Routledge, 2017) p.96.

14 In what reads like a witty riposte to Bourdieu, Alain Badiou elucidates in *Theory of the Subject* how the enumeration of cultural markers, and collapse of them into each other between members of classes, cannot suffice alone in itself as a palpable analysis of class structure and division: 'An objective consistency, reducible to a similarity of belonging, a law of the Same. The noun 'worker' designates this.

Do these 'workers' form a class? Yes, the sociologist will be pleased to find the special attributes, the similarities in clothing, attitudes, tastes, voting habits, and so on. The sociologist, in his bookkeeper's inventory, does not have to know about the exclusively differential nature of these similarities. It is clear that they regulate the same by way of the other, by way of the bourgeois, the professor, the farmer. The consistent interiority is missing. That which links the workers as class obviously cannot be summed up by the effects of their position. 'They' prefer *The Blue Danube* to Wagner? As a result, I consider them only as object *for another object*—the one who likes Wagner, the petit bourgeois; I do not exceed the algebra.

Rigorously speaking, one should say that here consistency is incon-sistent. For the structure of belonging of the workers to the labor market puts them in competition with one another. It disjoins them more so than it brings them together. You know what is *one* worker, you ignore what are two workers, as One.

This is the zero degree of the neighbourhood.' See Alain Badiou, *Theory of the Subject* [1982], trans. by Bruno Bosteels (London: Bloomsbury Academic, 2019) p.236.

15 For a developed interaction with this, see EDA Collective, 'Spectres Haunting Sectors: Crypto-currencies and Immaterial Conditions in Modern Class Division', https://everydayanalysis.net/2019/04/01/spectres-haunting-sectors-crypto-currencies-and-immaterial-conditions-in-modern-class-division/.

16 Ernst Parell [Wilhelm Reich], 'Objections to Mass Psychology – Part One' [1934], in Wilhelm Reich and Karl Teschitz, *Selected Sex-Pol Essays, 1934–1937: Articles from the 'Zeitschrift für Politische Psychologie und Sexualoekonomie'*, trans. unknown (London: Socialist Reproduction, 1973) p.94.

17 Reich, 'Dialectical Materialism and Psychoanalysis', in *Sex-Pol*, p.43.

18 Wilhelm Reich, 'Psychoanalysis in the Soviet Union' [1929], in ibid., pp.83–84.

19 Reich, 'Dialectical Materialism and Psychoanalysis', in ibid., p.42, n.44.

20 Similar was said in Reich's own time, of which he makes mention in reflections on his political beginnings in the late work *People in Trouble*, made up of a manuscript from 1937 with memoir material and commentary added in 1952. See Wilhelm Reich, *People in Trouble: The Emotional Plague of Mankind, Volume 2* [1953], trans. by Philip Schmitz (New York: Farrar, Straus and Giroux, 1976) p.19.

21 See Boris Johnson, 'The Male Sex is to Blame for the Appalling Proliferation of Single Mothers', *Spectator*, 19 August 1995, http://archive.spectator.co.uk/article/19th-august-1995/6/politics.

22 Marx, *Capital: Volume III*, p.570 [my italics].

23 Tove Ditlevsen, *Childhood* [1967], trans. by Tiina Nunnally (London: Penguin Classics, 2019) pp.7–8.

24 Ryan, *Class and Psychoanalysis*, p.177.

25 Viktor Tausk, 'Diagnostic Considerations Concerning the Symptomatology of the So-Called War Psychoses' [1916], trans, by Eric Mosbacher and Marius Tausk, in *Sexuality, War and Schizophrenia*, p.140, n.13.

26 See Alenka Zupančič, *What is Sex?* (Cambridge, MA: MIT Press, 2017) pp.30–34; and Wilhelm Reich, *The Sexual Revolution* [1936], trans. by Theodore P. Wolfe (London: Vision Press, 1972) rev. edn.

27 Ryan, *Class and Psychoanalysis*, p.100, n.2.

28 See Reich, 'Preface to the Third Edition, Revised and Enlarged' [1942], in *The Mass Psychology of Fascism*, p.17 and p.24, and p.112 in the work itself.

29 We might here read what distinguishes capitalistic and communistic investment against the psychoanalytic schema of disavowal: whilst capitalism is never calm, it always carries on; the issue with capitalism (which concentrates capital into circulations open only to capitalists whilst expropriating the proletariat, precariat, etc.) is that it concerns itself only with maximums possible in the present, with scant regard for what harm this may cause to others, now or to-come. In this regard, capitalism represents a disavowed

pessimism about the future; that is, whilst it could be construed as a preservative type of provision-building for the individual's future (i.e., beyond the recirculations of constant and variable capital, surplus-value could be saved, invested and thus multiplied, etc.), the harmful excess it creates in its reckless expansion creates negative effects (environmental, military, global, even financial, in terms of destabilisation drastically revaluing money and its abilities: i.e., sudden liquidations, bankruptcies, inflation hikes, etc.) on all inheritance beyond the individual's present, to say nothing of that on society. It is these negative effects that are disavowed (these effects are known to the capitalists, but all the same the capitalists carry on).

Communism and socialism, on the other hand, represent a disavowed optimism about the future in their concerning themselves with the oppressions of the present, which must be alleviated for the future to flourish. It is here that the communist's present ability to guiltlessly (or even pleasurably guiltily) *enjoy*—for example, as in the hedonism of excesses enjoyed by capitalists (despite whatever claims of 'abstinence' might still exist)—is disavowed, whether this is seen as sacrificially or responsibly.

30 See R. D. Laing, *The Divided Self: An Existential Study in Sanity and Madness* [1960] (London: Penguin Modern Classics, 2010) p.78.

31 Wilhelm Reich, 'What is Class Consciousness?' [1934], in *Sex-Pol*, p.345. See R. D. Laing, 'Liberation by Orgasm', *New Society*, 1968.

32 See, for example, Karl Marx and Frederick Engels, 'Address of the Central Committee to the Communist League (March 1850)', in Karl Marx, *The Revolutions of 1848: Political Writings, Volume 1*, ed. by David Fernbach, 3 vols (London: Verso, 2010) I, p.330. The theory is laid out over the course of Trotsky's works; see, specifically, Leon Trotsky, *The Permanent Revolution* and *Results and Prospects* [1930/1906], trans. by John G. Wright and Brian Pearce (London: Socialist Resistance, 2007), in particular, p.117, in which he describes as permanent 'a revolution whose every successive stage is rooted in the preceding one and which can end only in the complete liquidation of class society.' One might also think of Mao Zedong's 'continuous revolution'. For the influence, and adaptation, of Marx, Engels, and Trotsky's theories in Mao, see Matthew Galway, 'Permanent Revolution', in *Afterlives of Chinese Communism: Political Concepts from Mao to Xi*, ed. by Christian Sorace, Ivan Franceschini, and Nicholas Loubere (Acton, Australia: ANU Press and Verso Books) pp.181–188.

33 Reich, 'Dialectical Materialism and Psychoanalysis', in *Sex-Pol*, p.30.

34 Stuart Hall, 'Political Commitment' [1966], in *Selected Political Writings: 'The Great Moving Right Show' and Other Essays*, ed. by Sally Davison, David Featherstone, Michael Rustin and Bill Schwarz (Durham: Duke University Press, 2017) p.103.

35 For 'work-democracy', see Reich, *The Mass Psychology of Fascism*, p.346; for Lenin's reading of Friedrich Engels in this respect, see V. I. Lenin, *The State and Revolution* [1918], trans. by Robert Service (London: Penguin Classics, 1992) p.18, in which he discusses how revolutionary transition to communism will bring about the bourgeois democratic state 'ceasing of itself'.

Philosophically, it is worth turning to the distinction, made by Badiou (to the event of whose work fidelity is here inextricably linked) in the preface to *Logics of Worlds*, between 'democratic materialism' and 'materialist dialectic', if—with Badiou—'we agree that by 'dialectic', following Hegel, we are to understand that the essence of all difference is the third term that marks the gap between the two others. It is then legitimate to counter democratic materialism—this sovereignty of the Two (bodies and languages)—with a materialist dialectic, if by 'materialist dialectic' we understand the following statement, in which the Three supplements the reality of the Two: *There are only bodies and languages, except that there are truths.'* See Alain Badiou, *Logics of Worlds: Being and Event, 2* [2006], trans. by Alberto Toscano (London: Bloomsbury, 2013) p.4.

Appendix

At the beginning of the second chapter, we indicated two types of topology: the Möbial and the Borromean. These are two distinct topologies, as one concerns *knots* (from the unknot to the trefoil, and more complicated knots beyond), and the other *links* (the Borromean link, beyond which there are other types). The question as to whether the two types of structure are, or can be, directly connected, or whether one is derivable from the other, might here arise.

Jean-Gérard Bursztein hypothesises that the topologies are connected, in his work *The Unconscious, Its Space-Time*—or, rather, that unconscious structure is 'at the same time Mœbian and Borromean'— but suggests 'that in this problematic *the Mœbian-Borromean potentialities* are structural properties of the unconscious which [...] cannot be situated in the spaces of representation under which this structure can be approached', leaving the 'problem concerning the[ir] topological concept' open.[1] In this work, Bursztein postulates that the 'subspace' of the hole in the middle of the Borromean link creates a curvilinear triangle, formed from the crossing of each ring ('S' crossing 'I'; 'R' crossing 'S'; and 'R' crossing 'I', in the notation of the three orders, for example), then hints at the potentialities of conceptualising a thrice half-twisted Möbius strip within this space.

Working backwards from a 1.5-twist Möbius strip can in fact arrive us at a Borromean link via a series of cuts. This is a description of the experiment and its results that led to this discovery, in stages, with photographs depicting the methodology.

1   Take a 1.5-twist Möbius strip. This one (Figure A.1) has been created from paper, and shaded in the photograph, for the purpose of more easily describing elements of the structure.

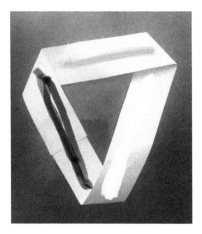

Figure A.1 1.5 Möbius strip.

2   The Borromean link, which—as well as from three tori (rings)—can be made from three linked bands, or unknots, would therefore, in such an instance, be depictable, flattened, by each band having four flattening-points, creating a continuous loop for each. However: initially in this construction, a fifth half-twist will be added to each band (which can later 'dissolve', as described in stage 4) so as to maintain the circular band shape as it connects to the Möbius strip. Figures A.2–A.4 show the addition of one band at a time, with the Borromean crossings, around the central Möbius strip.

3   On each of the Borromean bands three of the flattening-points are at right-angles, the last two at the ends of the bands are at angles equivalent to those of the tips of the Möbius strip (roughly so, in the photographs); for ease of reference, we might designate the Möbius strip a 45°–45°–90° triangle here. The five half-twists in each band create the Möbiality of each, and the flattening-points at the ends are folded over—and under—themselves so as to match the surface(s) of the Möbius strip; i.e., in Figure A.2, the flattening-point on the band adjacent to the bottom of the left-hand side of the picture—which we will label (1)—folds over itself at roughly a 45° angle, and that adjacent to the leftmost area of the bottom side (2) folds under itself similarly (likewise with the other shaded bands in the following pictures, with the band in the second representing the 90° angle, and that in the third the other 45° angle). Thus, (1) emulates the 'overside' part of the tip of the Möbius strip and

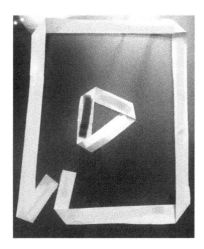

Figure A.2 Construction (1).

Figure A.3 Construction (2).

(2) the 'underside' part. (1) can then be glued to the upperside of the brightly shaded element of the Möbius strip, and (2) to the underside of the darkly shaded element, and the same process repeated for all the bands (with whether they attach 'over' or 'under' determining the crossing points), as in Figure A.5.

Figure A.4 Construction (3).

Figure A.5 Rosiform Möbial knot.

4   Once all the loose ends are connected, the Möbius strip remains entire in the middle of this structure. One is then required to cut along the fold at each of the Möbius strip's flattening-points, freeing up the complete structure: a single Möbius strip, of 15 half-twists (the three of the Möbius strip have 'dissolved' into the structure, by being cut), in a rosiform knot of nine crossings (and bearing a resemblance to the Borromean link). If the middle of this knot is then cut out (along the three-dotted lines in Figure A.6), the equivalent folds at the loose ends of each band can then merge back into

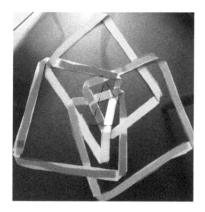

Figure A.6 Removal of central Möbius strip creating Borromean link.

right-angled flattening-points, creating complete bands, interlinked in the Borromean manner.

5 In regard to the rosiform knot, what is of interest is whether, in 'standing the structure on its side'—i.e., unflattening the whole strip—it could collapse into itself via self-intersections, in a requisite dimensionality, so as to sustain both the Möbius strip and the Borromean link at once. Determining this, however, is beyond the remit of this work, and my current capabilities.

In all topological instances within this short book, the experiments have been heuristically carried out, and descriptively put into a language lacking a proper mathematical basis, in which case the author asks the diligent reader's indulgence for errors unavoidable in the exceptional circumstances.

Note

1 See Jean-Gérard Bursztein, *The Unconscious, Its Space-Time: Aristotle, Lacan, Poincaré* [2017], trans. by Richard Klein (Paris: Hermann Éditeurs, 2020) p.11, p.64, and p.66, n.1.

Index

For Product Safety Concerns and Information please contact our EU
representative GPSR@taylorandfrancis.com
Taylor & Francis Verlag GmbH, Kaufingerstraße 24, 80331 München, Germany